CAMBRIDGE LIBRARY COLLECTION
Books of enduring scholarly value

Cambridge

The city of Cambridge received its royal charter in 1201, having already been home
to Britons, Romans and Anglo-Saxons for many centuries. Cambridge University
was founded soon afterwards and celebrates its octocentenary in 2009. This series
explores the history and influence of Cambridge as a centre of science, learning,
and discovery, its contributions to national and global politics and culture, and its
inevitable controversies and scandals.

Bibliotheca Pepysiana

Samuel Pepys (1633-1703) was a student of Magdalene College, Cambridge, and
bequeathed his personal library of 3000 volumes to the College on condition that
the contents remained intact and unaltered; they remain there, in his original
bookcases, to this day. In the early twentieth century, a project to produce a
complete catalogue was begun, and four volumes were published between 1914
and 1940. Volume 2 contains a general introduction to the library and its history,
including extracts from Pepys's diary, will, and accounts. It then lists and describes
the early printed books, with notes as to special features, other extant copies and
publication history, among them several liturgical books in the Sarum rite and
1557 editions of Malory's La morte d'Arhur and the works of Thomas More. It
also includes an index of printers. This catalogue remains a valuable resource for
researchers in early publishing history and seventeenth-century studies.

Cambridge University Press has long been a pioneer in the reissuing of out-of-print titles from its own backlist, producing digital reprints of books that are still sought after by scholars and students but could not be reprinted economically using traditional technology. The Cambridge Library Collection extends this activity to a wider range of books which are still of importance to researchers and professionals, either for the source material they contain, or as landmarks in the history of their academic discipline.

Drawing from the world-renowned collections in the Cambridge University Library, and guided by the advice of experts in each subject area, Cambridge University Press is using state-of-the-art scanning machines in its own Printing House to capture the content of each book selected for inclusion. The files are processed to give a consistently clear, crisp image, and the books finished to the high quality standard for which the Press is recognised around the world. The latest print-on-demand technology ensures that the books will remain available indefinitely, and that orders for single or multiple copies can quickly be supplied.

The Cambridge Library Collection will bring back to life books of enduring scholarly value across a wide range of disciplines in the humanities and social sciences and in science and technology.

Bibliotheca Pepysiana

*A Descriptive Catalogue of the Library of
Samuel Pepys*

VOLUME 2: GENERAL INTRODUCTION AND
EARLY PRINTED BOOKS TO 1558

EDWARD GORDON DUFF
F. SIDGWICK

CAMBRIDGE
UNIVERSITY PRESS

CAMBRIDGE UNIVERSITY PRESS

Cambridge New York Melbourne Madrid Cape Town Singapore São Paolo Delhi

Published in the United States of America by Cambridge University Press, New York

www.cambridge.org
Information on this title: www.cambridge.org/9781108002042

© in this compilation Cambridge University Press 2009

This edition first published 1914
This digitally printed version 2009

ISBN 978-1-108-00204-2

BIBLIOTHECA PEPYSIANA.

PART II.—GENERAL INTRODUCTION *and*
EARLY PRINTED BOOKS TO 1558.

NOTE.

Not more than 500 copies of the complete Catalogue will be issued; but owing to the special appeal made by this and one or two of the subsequent Parts, a limited number of extra copies of such Parts will be printed for independent sale.

The Illustrations, consisting of photographic fac-similes, will be issued in a portfolio as a separate Part.

BIBLIOTHECA PEPYSIANA

A DESCRIPTIVE CATALOGUE
OF THE LIBRARY OF
SAMUEL PEPYS

PART II.—GENERAL INTRODUCTION (F. Sidgwick)

AND

EARLY PRINTED BOOKS TO 1558

By E. GORDON DUFF

—

LONDON:

SIDGWICK & JACKSON, LTD.

MCMXIV

BIBLIOTHECA PEPYSIANA.

General Introduction.

§1.—CHARACTER OF THE LIBRARY.

THE Library here catalogued consists of nearly three thousand volumes collected by Samuel Pepys the Diarist (1632–1703), and now the property in perpetual trust of the Master and Fellows of Magdalene College, Cambridge. It is unique in several respects: it may be confidently stated that no other collection of books has remained so nearly in the condition in which it was left by its original owner. Save, perhaps, for a few volumes added or completed by his executor, after his death and by the instructions of his will, every volume was selected by Samuel Pepys. The great majority of the volumes are in a uniform binding; all bear some mark of his care; and the whole Library is stored in presses designed by him, on a system for which he alone was primarily responsible. With the greatest forethought for its future, he bequeathed it under conditions which prevent any additions, and have almost succeeded in preventing any losses.

In character it is, for a private Library, remarkably heterogeneous. Were the *Diary* non-existent, and were no other source of knowledge available, a judgement of Pepys's character formed upon a consideration of the contents of his Library would reveal him to have been a man of great breadth of interest and catholicity of taste, an inquisitive scholar

A

conversant with more languages than his own, and a person in whom a
a love of order and neatness in detail was paramount.

§ 2.—HISTORY OF THE LIBRARY.

The earliest hint of Pepys's interest in books occurs, as might be
expected, in the first pages of his *Diary*: " I paid Mrs. Michell, my
bookseller " (Jan. 23, 1659–60).   It should be recollected that the *Diary*
covers only nine of the seventy years of his life, from his twenty-seventh
to his thirty-sixth year.   In his record of nearly 3,500 days there are to be
found about five hundred references to books and to his growing Library.
He notes books that he read, books that he bought, books that he saw or
" turned over " on the stalls in the Temple or Westminster Hall, and
books that he lent, borrowed, or otherwise acquired.   He refers constantly
to the booksellers with whom he dealt, gives the prices he paid for books
and bindings, and details the methods he employed for storing, arranging,
and cataloguing his purchases.

The following extracts from the *Diary* show the gradual growth of the
Library during the years 1663–1669, and the development of Pepys's
methods of librarianship :—

1663. *Aug. 10.* Whereas before my delight was in multitude of books, and spending
money in that and buying alway of other things, now that I am become a better husband,
and have left off buying, now my delight is in the neatness of everything, and so cannot
be pleased with anything unless it be very neat, which is a strange folly.

1664. *Dec. 31.* This Christmas I judged it fit to look over all my papers and books ;
and to tear all that I found either boyish or not to be worth keeping, or fit to be seen.

1664–5. *Jan. 18.*   To my bookseller's, and there did give thorough direction for the
new binding of a great many of my old books, to make my whole study of the same
binding, within very few.

Feb. 3.   In my way taking my books from binding from my bookseller's.   My bill
for the rebinding of some old books to make them suit with my study, cost me, besides
other new books in the same bill, £3 ; but it will be very handsome.

Feb. 5.   Down to my chamber, among my new books, which is now a pleasant sight
to me to see my whole study almost of one binding.

1665–6. *Feb. 12.* Then to my bookseller's, and there received some books I have new bought, and here late choosing some more to new bind, having resolved to give myself £10 in books.

1666. *July 23.* Then comes Sympson, the Joyner; and he and I with great pains contriving presses to put my books up in: they now growing numerous, and lying one upon another on my chairs, I lose the use to avoyde the trouble of removing them when I would open a book.

Aug. 10. To Sympson, the joiner, and I am mightily pleased with what I see of my presses for my books, which he is making for me.

Aug. 13. I to Paul's Churchyard, to treat with a bookbinder, to come and gild the backs of all my books, to make them handsome, to stand in my new presses, when they come.

Aug. 17. I find one of my new presses for my books brought home, which pleases me mightily. With Sympson the joyner home to put together the press.

Aug. 24. Comes Sympson to set up my other new presses[1] for my books . . . So all the afternoon till it was quite dark hanging things, that is my maps and pictures and draughts, and setting up my books.

Aug. 31. Much pleased to-day with thoughts of gilding the backs of all my books alike in my new presses.

Sept. 28.[2] Comes . . . the bookbinder to gild the backs of my books. I got the glass of my book-presses to be done presently.

Oct. 3. Then home, to set up all my folio books, which are come home gilt on the backs, very handsome to the eye. . . . After dinner the bookbinder come, and I sent by him some more books to gild.

Oct. 6. Home, and set up my little books in one of my presses come home gilt, which pleases me mightily.

Oct. 9. To set my remainder of my books gilt in order.

Dec. 17. Spent the evening in fitting my books, to have the number set upon each, in order to my having an alphabet of my whole, which will be of great ease to me.

Dec. 19. I to my chamber, and there to ticket a good part of my books, in order to the numbering of them for my easy finding them to read as I have occasion.

Dec. 20. To bed, after having finished the putting of little papers upon my books to be numbered hereafter.

(1.) This seems to indicate that more than two presses were made at this time; but *cf.* the reference to "my two presses" under Jan. 10, 1667–8.

(2.) This is the first reference to his Library after the Fire of London, during which he removed his "money, and plate, and best things" to Sir W. Rider's at Bethnal Green, whither he went on Sept. 8th, after the Fire had abated, to fetch away his "journal-book, to enter for five days past."

Dec. 23 (Lord's day). . . . I to my chamber, and with my brother and wife did number all my books in my closet, and took a list of their names, which pleases me mightily, and is a jobb I wanted much to have done.

Dec. 25. With my brother reducing the names of all my books to an alphabet.

1666-7. *Jan. 8.* And there saw the catalogue of my books, which my brother had wrote out, now perfectly alphabeticall.

Feb. 2. My brother and I to write over once more with my own hand my catalogue of books, while he reads to me.[1]

1667-8. *Jan. 10.* The truth is, I have bought a great many books lately to a great value; but I think to buy no more till Christmas next, and those that I have will so fill my two presses,[2] that I must be forced to give away some to make room for them, it being my design to have no more at any time for my proper library than to fill them.

Feb. 2. (Lord's day). . . . I all day at home, and all the morning setting my books in order in my presses, for the following year, their number being much increased since the last, so as I am fain to lay by several books to make room for better.

Feb. 15. All the afternoon and evening [with Mrs. Pepys and Deb Willet] titleing of my books for the present year, and setting them in order.

Feb. 16 (Lord's day). All the morning making a catalogue of my books.

1668-9. *March 12.* . . . He [W. Howe] carried me to Nott's, the famous book-binder, that bound for my Lord Chancellor's Library; and here I did take occasion for curiosity to bespeak a book to be bound, only that I might have one of his binding.

May 24. Setting my brother to making a catalogue of my books.

The last entry is dated just a week before the end of the *Diary.* In the course of the whole *Diary* from 1650–60 to 1669 he mentions the names of about one hundred and twenty-five books that he read, and records the purchase[3] or gift of about one hundred and fifty. Many—but by no means all—of the latter are still to be found in the Library.

The history of the Library between this point, when Pepys's two presses contained it—proving it to have then consisted of not more than five hundred volumes—and the date of his death, can be only partially reconstructed. The chief source of evidence is Pepys's correspondence with

---

(1.) This catalogue was finished on February 5.

(2.) *See* note to Aug. 24, 1666, above.

(3.) The prices, however, are seldom stated ; several times Pepys prefers to mention a lump sum, £10 or £5, as spent on books.

his friends, which continually testifies to his insatiable interest in books, engravings, and printed matter generally. Occasionally other evidence is available : there is a copy of the printed catalogue of the sale in 1682 of the library of Richard Smith containing the prices and purchasers' names ; and some of these books were purchased by or for Pepys and are still in his Library.[1] Among the correspondence there is a letter from Robert Scott the bookseller to Pepys, dated June 30, 1688, announcing that he is sending four books, for one of which Pepys had enquired, and subjoining a bill :—

" Campion, Hanmer, and Spencer, fol.	...		0 : 12 : 0
Harding's Chronicle, 4°	...	...	...	0 : 6 : 0
Pricaei Defens. Hist. Brit.		...	...	0 : 8 : 0
Shipp of Fooles, fol.	...	...	...	0 : 8 : 0
				1 : 14 : 0 "

These volumes are also in the Library, respectively Nos. **2000, 1442, 1165** and **2032.**

Purchase and gift, however, were not the only means by which Pepys contributed to his collection. In 1692 we find him writing to John Evelyn "in reference to that vast treasure of papers which I have had of yours so many years in my hands," and in 1700 the Admiralty, through its Secretary T. Burchett, demanded the return of "several books and papers still in your custody, particularly your public Letter Books." It is to be feared that in neither case was the whole lending restored. Certain books and prints, also, are recorded as having been presented to Pepys.

But in the main his Library was fairly bought in many markets.[2] He often gave commissions to friends who were travelling abroad ; and towards

---

(1.) See *The Library of Richard Smith,* an article by E. Gordon Duff in *The Library,* April, 1907. Nos. **1254**[3], *Wednesday's Fast,* and **1254**[6], *The Foundation of the Chapel of Walsingham,* each unique, changed hands at Smith's sale.

(2.) Rawl. MSS. A. 190, f. 146, is "Mr. Fowler's bill," dated from Seville, January 1, 1683–4, containing a dozen items.

the end of his life (1699–1700) he employed his nephew John Jackson, who was engaged on a two years' tour of the continent, including a long sojourn in Rome, to purchase quantities of prints and books. Writing to Evelyn on December 4, 1701, Pepys refers to "my two or three months' by-work of sorting and binding together my nephew's Roman marketings"; and, still acquisitive, adds "I shall struggle hard to give him leisure next summer to finish his travels in Holland."

Meanwhile, it is clear, he was an assiduous librarian. Some of the volumes in the Library still bear seven changes of press-mark, testifying to continual re-arrangement, or, as Pepys calls it, "adjustment." None of the catalogues or "alphabets" mentioned in the *Diary* survive, but the MS. catalogue made by John Jackson in 1705, *Supellex Literaria*, revises the "adjustment" to Michaelmas, 1700, and refers to the "last Adjustment, A.D. 1693."[1] During John Jackson's absence on the tour referred to above, Pepys employed as amanuensis and cataloguer Paul Lorrain, a scribe who had in 1681 dedicated to Pepys his translation into French of Tillotson's *The Protestant Religion Vindicated*, and in 1683 his translation into English of Pierre Muret's *Rites of funeral ancient and modern*; and in writing to his nephew on October 19, 1699, Pepys mentions the "necessity for transcribing my Alphabet and Catalogue"—obviously the forerunner of the *Supellex Literaria*. A list of one hundred and twenty-nine manuscripts belonging to Pepys, "varii quidem argumenti, sed praecipue de re navali, quae est Anglorum gloria ac praesidium," was included in Bernard's *Catalogi Librorum Manuscriptorum Angliae et Hiberniae*, Oxford, 1697, vol. ii, pp. 207–210. This is the "printed catalogue" to which William Nicholson, Archdeacon of Carlisle, refers, in writing to Pepys, June 14, 1700, with "enquiries about some of your MSS."

Almost on the same day Pepys's familiar correspondent Thomas Gale, then Dean of York, wrote to him :—

(1.) *See also* No. 2700, "*Sea*" *Manuscripts*, p. 21.

" I wish your cousin [*sc.* nephew], Mr. Jackson, were now with you ; his good company, handyness in turning your books, and other ministrations, would yield you much ease.   When you shall think fit to make your last will and settlement, I beg of you that you would be pleased to put all your rare collections (of which you have so many) into some one good hand."

This collocation is prophetic; for although Pepys, in his will[1] dated August 2, 1701, makes no mention of his library, in the codicil which he added on May 12, 1703, with the purpose of revoking his bequests to Samuel Jackson (who had " thought fit to dispose of himselfe in marriage against my positive advice and injunctions ") and of transferring the benefit to Samuel's younger brother John, there occurs the following clause :—

" Item, I will that my nephew John Jackson have the full and Sole possession and use of all my Collections of Books and papers contained in my Library (now remaining at Mr Hewers at Clapham or in any other place or places) during the Terme of his natural Life   And in case it shall not please God in his mercy to restore me to a Condition of prosecuting my thoughts, relating to a more perticular disposal and Settlement thereof My will and desire is that my said nephew John Jackson doe with all possible diligence betake himself to the dispatch of such pticulars as shall be remaining undone at the time of my decease towards the completion of my said Library according to the Scheme delivered to him for that purpose and intended to be hereunto annexed   And that he together with my Executor[2] and such of their friends as they shall judge fittest and best qualified to advise them herein doe faithfully and deliberately consider of the most effectual means for preserving the said Library intire in one body, undivided unsold and Secure against all manner of deminution damages and embesselments ; and finally disposed most suitably to my inclinations (declared likewise in the before mentioned Scheme) for the benefit of posterity."

After three other " Items," Pepys proceeds :—

" Item I further give unto my Servant David Milo, as a reward for his Extraordinary diligence and usefulness to me, in Several matters relating to my books, the Sum of twenty pounds upon condition nevertheless that he continue the space of halfe a year at the least after my decease in the Service of my nephew John Jackson at the wages of ten pounds per Ann. to assist him in the before mentioned perticulars, relating to the completion of my Library."

(1.)   Will and codicil were first printed in *Pepysiana*, the supplementary volume to the *Diary*, edited by H. B. Wheatley, 1899, pp. 251· 270.

(2.)   William Hewer, his faithful clerk, with whom Pepys had been residing at Clapham since 1700, in the house in which he died, May 26, 1703.

The codicil is thereafter signed, sealed, and witnessed, and immediately followed by :

"THE SCHEME REFERRED TO IN MY FOREGOING CODICIL RELATING TO THE COMPLETION AND SETTLEMENT OF MY LIBRARY, VIZ.ᵀ

FOR THE COMPLETION OF MY LIBRARY.

I will and require that the following perticulars be carefully punctually and with all possible diligence and dispatch performed and Executed by my nephew John Jackson after my decease vizt.

1st   That a general review be taken of my said Library compared with its Catalogue and all outlying books imediately lookt up and put into their places.

2ndly   That my Collections of Stamps[1] or any others which shall then be depending be finished, bound placed and properly entred in my Catalogue and Alphabet.

3rdly   That all Setts of Books contained in my said Library under the name of growing Tracts be compleated to the time of my Death and roome provided for the further volumes of my Lord Clarendon's History now under the press.[2]

4thly   That Gronovius's Sett of Greek Antiquities lately publish't[3] be forthwith bought and added thereto and any other considerable Desiderata supplyed at the discretion of my said nephew with the advice of his learned ffriends.

5thly   That this being done my said Library be closed and from thenceforward noe Additions made thereto.

6thly   That the whole number and bulke of my books being soe ascertained one or more new presses be provided for the convenient containing them soe as to be neither too much crowded nor Stand too loose.

7thly   That my Arms or Crest or Cypher be Stampt in Gold on the outsides of the Covers of every booke admitting thereof.

8thly   That their placing as to heighth be strictly reviewed and where found requiring it more nicely adjusted.

9thly   That soe soon as their order shall be thus fixt the whole be new numbred from the lowest to the highest.

10thly   That the said new number be Stampt on a piece of Redd Leather fixt at the head of the back of every book where now the guilt paper is.

(1.)   *i.e.*, "Raccolta di Stampe Romane," the collection of prints, **Nos. 2955** (missing)**–2961.**

(2.)   Nos. **2944-6** ; the Oxford edition in three vols. folio, 1702–4.

(3.)   Nos. **2767-79** : *Thesaurus Graecarum antiquitatum,* 12 vols. folio, Lugduni Batavorum, 1697–1702.

11[thly] That all the Additaments with their new numbers be then properly incerted in the bodies of the Catalogue and Alphabet and there elegantly and finally transcribed to remaine unalterable and for ever accompany the said Library.

12[thly] Lastly That as farr as any room shall be left for further improvements or embellishments to my books by Ruling, Elegant writing or Indexing the same be done at the discretion and convenience of my said nephew.

On the following day, May 13, 1703, a second codicil included instructions[1] " For the further Settlement & Preservation of my said Library, after the death of my Nephew John Jackson," beginning :—

" I do hereby declare That could I be sure of a constant Succession of Heirs from my said Nephew qualified like himself for the use of such a Library I should not entertain a thought of its ever being Alienated from them.　But this uncertainty considered with the infinite paines and time and cost employed in my Collecting Methodizing and reducing the same to the State wherein it now is I cannot but be greatly Solicitous that all possible provision should be made for its unalterable preservation and perpetual Security against the ordinary ffate of such Collections falling into the hands of an incompetent heir and thereby of being sold dissipated or imbezelled."

The testator therefore proceeds to state his "present thoughts and prevailing inclinations in this matter viz[t]. :—

" 1st That after the death of my said nephew my said Library be placed and for ever Settled in one of our Universities and rather in that of Cambridge than Oxford.　2[dly] And rather in a private College there than the publick Library.　3[dly] And in the Colleges of Trinity or Magdalen preferable to All others.　4[thly] And of these two Caeteris paribus, rather in the latter for the Sake of my own and nephews Education therein.　5[thly] That in which soever of the two it is a faire roome be provided therein on purpose for it and wholly and soly appropriated thereto.　6[thly] And if in Trinity, That the said room be contiguous and to have communication with the new Library there.　7[thly] And if in Magdalen That it be in the new building there, and any part thereof at my nephews election.　8[thly] That my said Library be continued in its present form and noe other books mixt therewith Save what my Nephew may add to them of his own Collecting in distinct presses.　9[thly] That the said roome and books so placed and adjusted be called by the name of Bibliotheca Pepysiana.　10[thly] That this Bibliotheca Pepysiana be under the sole power and custody of the Master of the College for the time being who shall neither himself convey nor Suffer to be conveyed by others any of the said books from thence to any other place except to his own Lodge in the said College nor there have more than ten of them at a time and that of those also a strict entry be made and account kept of the time of their having been taken out and returned, in a booke to be provided and remain in the

---

(1.) Rawl. MSS. D. 923, f. 296, etc., is apparently Pepys's original draft of these instructions.

said Library for that only purpose.   11^thly That before my said Library be put into the possession of either of the said Colleges, that College for which it shall be designed first enter into Covenants for performance of the foregoing articles.   12^thly And that for a yet further Security herein the said two Colleges of Trinity and Magdalen have a Reciprocal Check upon one another.   And that the College which shall be in present possession of the said Library be subject to an Annual visitation from the other and to the forfeiture thereof to the like possession and Use of the other upon Conviction of any breach of their said Covenants.   S. Pepys."

Within a fortnight of signing the above, Pepys died, and the Library passed into the hands of William Hewer and John Jackson.   Pepys had been aware, as he states in his will quoted above, that not all the Library was in Hewer's house at Clapham.   As a matter of fact, more than seventy volumes of his MSS., mainly correspondence, remained at York Buildings and were lost to Cambridge; ultimately they were secured by Dr. Rawlinson, and were included in his bequest to the Bodleian Library, Oxford.[1]

Hewer and Jackson lost no time in carrying out Pepys's stipulations. Among the Rawlinson MSS.[2] is their declaration, dated April 20, 1704, rehearsing in abstract the terms of the will and codicils, and appointing that the Library "to the just number of Three Thousand volumes contained in Twelve wainscot Presses, and one Table, Together with the said Presses and three other Volumes containing a Catalogue, Alphabet and Classical distribution thereof" shall after the decease of John Jackson belong to "Magdalen Colledge," provided they will agree to Pepys's conditions, or failing Magdalene to Trinity, with the same proviso.

The "Catalogue, Alphabet and Classical distribution" (*i.e.*, hand-list, catalogue, and subject-index) are still part of the Library.   On p. 165 of *Supellex Literaria*, Pepys's "catalogue" or list of books "adjusted to Michaelmas 1700", is the following note:

"Total 2474.   Review'd & finally Placed August 1st 1705: No one of ye 2474 Books contained in the foregoing Catalogue being then wanting.   J. Jackson.   vid. rest

(1.) See *Notes and Queries*, 2nd Ser., v. 142 (1858).   Rawlinson MSS. A. 170 to 240 is a series of Pepysian MSS.
(2.) Rawl. D. 923, f. 293 *et seqq.*

of ye Library in Additament. Catalogue consisting of 526 Books more, making the whole Number just 3000. J. Jackson."

William Hewer died in 1715, and John Jackson in March, 1722–3. Little is known about the Library during the twenty years in which the latter enjoyed its possession, but on two occasions the journalists of the day appear to have obtained some information from it.[1]

A year after Jackson's death, the Library was transferred from Clapham to Cambridge. The following entry[2] in the Magdalene College books proves that the Magdalene authorities welcomed the bequest and submitted to the conditions attached to it :—

"July 1724. Received of the R^t. Honble. Arthur Earl of Anglesea[3] the sum of two hundred pounds, of which was expended in removing and settling Mr. Pepys's Library as follows :

For Boxes, Workmen, Necessary Expences and Carriage from Clapham to London ...	22—18—11
Carriage to Cambridge	18—03—10
Chamber Income	26—05 — 0
Wainscoting the Chamber, etc.	44—18 — 7
Necessary Expences	02—11 — 8
Herald Painter	02—02 -- 0
	£117 — 0 — 0 "

(1.) In June, 1707, a periodical entitled *The Muses Mercury* printed the now famous poem of *The Nutbrown Maid* from Pepys's collection, with the following preface : " We may be ask'd, perhaps, how we came by this Rarity : We can give a very good Account of it, and therefore are not afraid of such a question. It is known to most People conversant with Books, and Bookish Men, that the late *Samuel Pepys*, Esq ; who was so long Secretary to the Admiralty, made a Collection of all the Ballads that he could procure, from *Chevy Chase* to *T——m D————y's* [Tom D'Urfey's]. At the Head of this Collection was this Poem of the *Nut-brown* Maid ; not that it is a *Ballad* ; but an Allegorical *Poem*, with more Design in it than many of our late Odes." In 1708 an account of the Library appeared in *The Monthly Miscellany, or Memoirs for the Curious*, vol. ii, 178 ; a copy of this, made by Rawlinson, is on f. 300 of Rawl. MS. D. 923.

(2.) Previously printed by Willis and Clark, *Architectural History of the University of Cambridge*, ii. 373 ; and H. B. Wheatley, *Pepysiana*, 34.

(3.) The Earl of Anglesey was the heir of Pepys's former master, the Treasurer of the Navy who was suspended from his office in 1688.

The transference of the Library to Cambridge is recorded in *Parker's London News*, no. 887, July 24, 1724.[1]

The above mentioned "chamber," in which the books were deposited on their arrival, occupied the whole of the first floor over the arcade in the "new building," for a room in which Pepys, as we have seen, stipulated in his second codicil. This building is that which still forms the back of the second court in Magdalene, a beautiful piece of architecture with an arcade of five arches flanked by two wings; "BIBLIOTHECA PEPYSIANA 1724" is inscribed above the centre arch, below the middle one of the five windows which lit the Library's first resting-place in Magdalene. Pepys himself had contributed £60 towards the cost of this "new building," the foundations of which were laid in 1677; his arms and motto, *Mens cuiusque is est quisque*, appear with the inscription above quoted, and are no doubt the work of the "Herald Painter" who received two guineas in the account.

Very little information regarding the Library during the next hundred years can be recovered. In 1728, four years after the arrival of the books at Cambridge, the *Diary*, as Mr. Wheatley has shown,[2] was observed, and came near to being investigated and perhaps deciphered, by Peter Leicester, a correspondent of John Byrom the poet, who was interested in Pepys's hobby of tachygraphy or shorthand.

In 1748 the Magdalene College books contain a note of the following expenditure on the Pepysian Library :—

1748.	Sept. 17th.	Pd for transcribing ye Catalogue	1 .. 3 .. 6
	Oct. 4th.	Pd for Paper for Do & Binding	0 .. 13 .. 4
	Oct 21st.	Pd Glasiers Bill	2 .. 6 .. 7
	Novr. ye 23.	Painters Bill	4 .. 7 .. 5½
			8 .. 10 .. 10½

(1.) See *Notes and Queries*, 2nd Ser., ix. 158.

(2.) *Pepysiana*, 73-4.

Naturally enough, acquaintance with the contents of the Library was restricted to a few historians and scholars : Bishop Percy, in enumerating in the preface to his *Reliques* (first published in 1765) the collections of broad-side ballads on which he had drawn, places first the Pepysian Library, and acknowledges the assistance of Mr. Blakeway, "late fellow of Magdalen College ;" in 1780, Horace Walpole quotes in a letter of December 19 to the Rev. Mr. Cole a reference to the Library made in " Mr. Gough's new edition ;" and in 1811 the Index to Pepys's "Prints and Drawings relating to London" was copied for Mr. Charles Richardson of Covent Garden.[1]

After remaining in the large "chamber" until 1834, by which time the *Diary* was published and the name of Pepys familiar, the Library was moved.   Under date May 7, 1833, the Magdalene College Order Book makes record :—

" The following answer has been received from Trinity to an application made by the Master respecting the proposed removal of the Pepysian Library—

" May 6, 1833. —Agreed by the Master and Seniors that the consent of the College be given to the removal of the Books &c. of the Pepysian Library from their present situation in Magdalene College to an appartment in the Master's Lodge of the same College.

Chr. Wordsworth M.C."

On Jan. 22, 1834, the Magdalene College Order Book records the decision :

" That the Pepysian Library should be moved into the new Master's Lodge, the space it now occupies being converted into College Rooms."

The new Master's Lodge was finished in 1837, but fifteen years elapsed before the Library was transferred ; the Order Book states :

" May 19, 1849.   In conformity with the College Order of Jan. 22, 1834, the Pepysian Library has been removed into the Master's Lodge."

Finally, in 1854, the Library was once more removed into a fire-proof room on the first floor of the south wing of the building in which it had been first deposited, and here it has since remained.

(1.) This is now Bodleian MS. 30, 734.

§3.—Description of the Library.

1. The Presses.

The three thousand volumes are preserved in the twelve presses and Pepys's writing-table, the pedestals of which are converted into cases for large books, and on the top of which is a double desk containing the collections of Prints, etc. The disposition of presses and table will be seen in the accompanying plan. The spaces caused by the overhang of the cornices between presses 1 and 2, 2 and 3, 9 and 10, and 11 and 12 are fitted with mirror-fronted cupboards.

Each press consists of an oblong case at the bottom, about 4 feet broad, 19 inches high, and 20–23 inches deep. This is fronted with two drop-shutters of glass-panes in oak frames, sliding in grooves. Upon it stands the upper part of the press, the interior of which consists of a pair of cases about 5 feet 9 inches high, and together rather less in breadth than the floor-case. The upper pair of cases each contain four shelves, and are protected by a pair of glass doors.

The system of press-marking is as follows. In each press the shelves are numbered from the top downwards, shelves 1, 2, 3, and 4 being in the upper part, and shelf 5 being the floor-case. The upper part being vertically divided into two halves, the left side is numbered 1 and the right 2 ; this does not apply to shelf 5, as the floor-case is not divided. Shelves 2, 3 and 4 each contain two rows of books, the front row being referred to as *a*, the back as *b*.

Thus the press-mark "8. 3a. 2" signifies "press 8, shelf 3, front row, right-hand side."

2. Method of Arrangement.

The key to Pepys's method of arranging his books is found in his instruction to Jackson "that their placing as to heighth be strictly reviewed and where found requiring it more nicely adjusted." The whole Library is therefore arranged according to the size of the volumes. The largest of

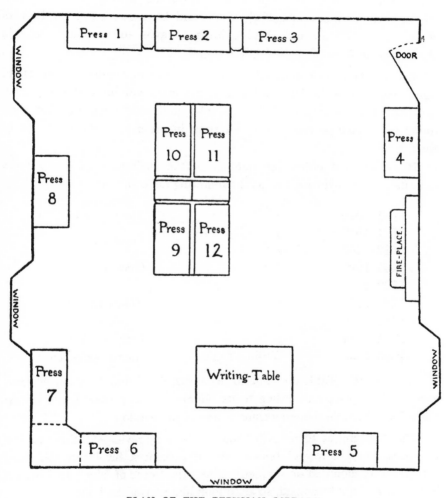

PLAN OF THE PEPYSIAN LIBRARY.

all, as stated above, are kept in and upon the writing-table; the next largest in the floor-cases (shelf 5); folios and large quartos at the back of shelves 2, 3 and 4; and small quartos, octavos and smaller books in shelf 1 and in front of shelves 2, 3 and 4.

Every volume is numbered. The numbers run regularly from left to right, beginning at the left-hand end of the front row of shelf 4 in press 1 (*i.e.*, No. 1 is press-marked "1. 4a. 1"), and continuing on that shelf round the twelve presses before restarting in press 1 on the front row of shelf 3.

It follows that either the number or the shelf-mark of any volume indicates its approximate size, as the following table shows:—

Nos.	Shelf.	Row.	Sizes (approx.).
1– 520	4	*a*	16mos, 12mos, etc.
521–1017	3	*a*	} Octavos.
1018–1455	2	*a*	
1456–1827	1		Quartos.
1828–2191	2	*b*	
2192–2485	3	*b*	} Folios and quartos.
2486–2710	4	*b*	
2711–2964	5		Large books.
2965–3000	Writing-Table.		Guard-books, etc.

A complete "Table directing to the Press, Shelf, and Division wherein each Book is placed according to its Number" was prepared, and is now framed and hung in the embrasure of one of the windows.

The "placing as to heighth" was so "strictly reviewed" that in a few instances, where a row of books did not present a level top, the short volumes were mounted on wooden "stilts," the fronts of which are covered in leather and gold-stamped, so as to look like part of the book.

It has been shown above that John Jackson's final "adjustment" of the Library in 1705 accounted for exactly 3,000 volumes, of which 2,474 are listed in the *Supellex Literaria*, and 526 in the *Additamenta*. In the former, both the previous serial-number and the new (or final) one are given; in the latter, which deals only with "such Books as have been added to my Library since ye last Adjustment thereof, 1700," few books, of course, possess a previous number.

It can be assumed that the figure 2474 correctly represented 2474 volumes in 1705; but the *Additamenta* does not, and never did, comprise 526 volumes. Jackson's task included re-numbering the whole Library in one series (the number is written in red ink at the top of the inside of the front cover of each volume); but as he was at the same time rearranging and rebinding various series of Pepys's collections, he left open, at the beginning or end of these, several figures. Thus, in the *Additamenta* of 526 figures, 29 have no title set against them.[1]

At least two, however, of these 29 blanks represent volumes that must have been missing when Jackson concluded his task[2]; possibly there were others wanting. No. **2848** is left blank in the *Additamenta*, No. **2849** being *S. P.'s Letters, Admiralty, vol. II;* but there is a previous serial-number against the blank, proving that Vol. I had previously been in the Library. Similarly No. **2955** is blank, though it should represent *Raccolta di Stampe, vol. I,* as may be discovered from another source of information.

This source is a list, following the *Supellex Literaria,* entitled :—" Here follow the Deleta. Containing An Account of such Books, as having been laid-aside or removed since the last Adjustment, or shall be after this; stand lined-out in ye praeced.^{ng} Catalogue, of Michaelm.^{s} 1700. With the Occasion of ye Same."

The "occasion" of altering the position of most of the hundred volumes in this list of *Deleta* is recorded as "Removed to a juster [or

---

(1.) For example, Nos. **1918-1931** are fourteen volumes of Du Pin's *Nouvelle Bibliothèque des auteurs ecclesiastiques* (Paris, 1690-1703), for which Jackson had left open eighteen numbers. Therefore **1932-1935** are left blank.

(2.) It may be noticed that he only declares that none of the 2474 volumes of the *Supellex Literaria* are wanting.

properer] place." Many others "give way" to another edition, "later," "older," or "fairer"; among these a *Missale Romanum ad Usum Sarum* gives way to a fairer edition[1] of 1520 (No. **2795**). Sixteen volumes are "ejected," some as being single works contained in a collected edition, some as duplicates—among them a volume of Pocket Tables and Charts, "being King Henry 8th's own Book, printed and MSS.," similar to that which bears Sir Francis Drake's name (No. **1**). Two volumes are marked "Vnbound, to be made (with Other Pieces) a 1st Vol. of Stampe Romane."

4. MISSING BOOKS.

The Pepysian Library, then, as completed by Jackson in 1705, may be presumed to have consisted of 2,971 volumes :—

> 2,474   being listed in *Supellex Litereria.*
>   497   *i.e.*, 526 listed in *Additamenta*, minus 29 blanks.
> ————
> 2,971

Between December, 1906, and February, 1907, I examined every volume in the Library, noting all the missing numbers between 1 and 3000. There proved to be thirty-six of these, of which twenty-nine are accounted for above; the remaining seven represent volumes lost from the Library since it left Jackson's hands. The following is a list of the books, the titles being given as they appear in *Supellex Literaria* and *Additamenta* :—

No.	Title.
130.	Bale's Martyrdom of Sir John Oldcastle. / Segar's Disswasive from a Court-Life—about 1549.
234.	Sr. Ken. Digby's Discourse of the Sympathetick Powder, in an Assembly at Montpelier.
300.	The Affair of ye Queen of Scots, in Scotch—1566.
458.	Skelton (Poet Laureat) his Satyr against Woolsey; printed in the Cardinal's Life-time.

(1.) This, R. Pynson's *Missale*, folio, is described by Mr. Gordon Duff (*Catalogue of Early Printed Books*, p. 46) as "perhaps the finest production of the early English press."

No.	Title.
549.	English Liturgy in French.
825.	{ A MSS List of his Majesties Fleet (of his own & hired ships) imployed against Holland 1671, 1672, & 1673.
2069.	{ Accot. of the Rise, Progress, & present State of ye Troubles in Virginia 1677 : With Proposals of the Proper Remedys thereto—MSS.

In the course of going through the Library, I came across a manuscript note of seven " Books wanting in Pepys's Library, Mar. 27. 1744 " ; five were subsequently marked as returned, the other two being Nos. **300** and **825** in the above list.

The missing printed books cannot be identified with certainty from the titles given above.

130¹ is apparently *A brefe Chronycle concernynge the examinacyon and death of . . . syr. J. Oldecastell the Lorde Cobham,* by John Bale, Bishop of Osscry ; printed 1544, second edition about 1560.

130² perhaps by Francis Seager, author of the *School of Virtue,* 1557 ; Mr. R. B. McKerrow suggests that it may be Antonio de Guevara's *A Dispraise of the Life of a Courtier,* translated from the French version of Antony Alaygre by Sir Francis Bryan, and printed by Grafton in 1548.

234 was published in French and English in 1658 and in Latin in 1660.

300. The MS. note of Mar. 27, 1744, mentioned above, calls this " Buchanan's Affair of the Queen of Scots." Doubtless it was a copy of *Ane Detectioun of the Doingis of Marie Quene of Scottis.* Hazlitt, *Collections,* ii. 67, says John Day was the printer.

458 may be an edition of *Why come ye not to court ?* or *Colin Clout.*

F. SIDGWICK.

January, 1914.

EARLY PRINTED BOOKS TO 1558.

Catalogued by E. GORDON DUFF.

ARNOLD (RICHARD). Chronicle of London.

fol. [*Adriaen van Berghen. Antwerp*, 1503.]

Leaf 2ᵃ. IN this booke is | Conteyned the | names of yᵉ bay | lifs Custos ma | irs and Sherefs | of the cite of lon | dō from the ty- | me of king rich | ard the furst. *&* | also thartycles | of the Chartur | and libarties of | the same Cyte. | [*etc.*]. Ends leaf 131, col. 2, line 13. kyng and all the parlament in sigū [*sic*] | and tokyn off good loue and accorde | whiche was done.

Collation. a⁴, A⁸, B⁴, C–E⁸, F–Q⁶, R⁸, S–V⁶; 132 leaves. 40 lines. No headlines; with numbers to pages.

Leaf 1 blank, 2ᵃ–4ᵇ Index, 5ᵃ–12ᵃ List of Bailiffs, etc., 12ᵇ blank, 13ᵃ–131ᵃ Text, 131ᵇ, 132, blank. Wants leaves 75, 76, 77, 78, part of 98, 131, 132. [*B.L.*]   [1882.]

Though called a Chronicle the work is more in the nature of a merchant's common-place book containing miscellaneous recipes, examples of business letters and accounts, etc. In the middle between remarks on the customs of Antwerp and "the rekenyng to bey waris in flaundres" occurs the ballad of the Nutbrown Maid. The work was reprinted with additions about 1520 by Peter Treveris. Herbert III. 1746–1751.

ASSIZE OF BREAD.   4to. *Richard Bankes. London.*

Title. ⊄ Here begynnethe the boke named the assyse of | Bread what it ought to waye after the pryce of a | quarter of wheete. And also thassyse of al maner | of wood, lathe, bourde, tymbre, and the waight | of Butyre, and chese. Enprynted at the request of | Mychaell Englysshe and Johñ Rudstone alder- | men of the cyte of London. | [Woodcuts]. Leaf 12ᵇ *Colophon.* Finis. | Enprynted by Rychard Bākes | ⊄ Cum priuilegio.

Collation. A–C⁴; 12 leaves. 32 lines. No headlines or numbers to pages.

Leaf 1ᵃ Title, 1ᵇ Woodcuts, 2ᵃ–12ᵇ Text. [*B.L.*]   [1434¹⁰.]

c

On the title-page are four cuts of 1 Weighing bread, 2 Baking, 3 A dog watching a butter tub, and 4 Weighing wood. These are repeated on the verso of the page. From pages 6 to 21 two pages are read across and each pair have at the top two cuts, each divided into four compartments with little pictures of 1 The quarter of whete, 2 "A farthynge wastell, 3 A farthynge Symnell, 4 A farthynge whyte lofe, 5 A halfpeny whyte lofe, 6 A halfepeny wheten lofe, 7 A peny wheeten lofe, 8 A halfpeny housholde lofe."

John Rudstone was sheriff in 1522 and mayor in 1528: Michael English was sheriff in 1523.

This copy is printed on vellum and no other is known. Hartshorne, 238. Hazlitt I, 474. Sandars 132.

BAIF (LAZARE DE). De re navali, etc.
4to. *Robert Estienne. Paris,* 1549.
Title. Lazari Bayfii annota- | tiones in L.II. De captiuis, *&* postli- minio re- | uersis: in quibus tractatur de re nauali. | EIVSDEM ANNOTATIONES | in tractatum De auro *&* argento leg. quibus Vesti‐ | mentorum *&* Vasculorum genera explicantur. | Omnia ab ipso authore recognita *&* aucta. | ANTONII THYLESII DE CO | loribus libellus, à coloribus vestium non alienus. | LVTETIAE, | Ex officina Roberti Stephani, typographi Regii. | M.D.XLIX. | Ex priuilegio Regis. Leaf 174ᵃ
Colophon. EXCVDEBAT ROBERTVS STEPHANVS | TYPO- GRAPHVS REGIVS PA- | RISIIS, ANN. M.D.XLIX. | PRID. ID. SEPTEMB.
Collation. A–X⁸ Y⁶; 174 leaves. 31 lines. With headlines and numbers to pages.
Leaf 1ᵃ Title, 1ᵇ blank, 2ᵃ- 3ᵇ Dedication by Baif to Francis, 3ᵇ Letter of C. Stephanus, 4ᵃ–76ᵇ De re navali, 77ᵃ Title, 77ᵇ blank, 78ᵃ–79ᵇ Dedication to Cardinal John of Lorraine, 80 Vlpianus de auro, 81ᵃ–125ᵇ De re vestiaria, 126ᵃ Title, 126ᵇ blank, 127 Dedication to Antonio à Burgo, 128ᵃ–158ᵇ De vasculis, 159ᵃ Title, 159ᵇ Preface, 160ᵃ–168ᵇ De coloribus, 169ᵃ–173ᵇ Indices, 174ᵃ colophon, 174ᵇ blank. [*R.L.*]   [**1763.**]
Bound in handsome old red morocco, with book-plates of J. Jobert.

Twenty-eight extra plates have been inserted in this copy, eleven signed J. Damery Romae, four signed Romae 1552, and thirteen signed E. V. 1543 [Aeneas Vico].

——— De Re Navali Libellus. 8°. *Haeredes S. Vincentii. Lyons,* 1537.
Title. DE RE NA|VALI LIBELLVS IN|ADOLESCENTVLORVM BONA- | rum literarum studiosorū fauorem, | ex Bayfii uigiliis excerptus,

& | in breuem summulam faci- | litatis gratia redactus. | Addita ubique, puerorum causa, uulgari | uocabulorum significatione. | [Device] | LVGDVNI | APVD HAEREDES SIMONIS | VINCENTII | M.D. XXXVII.

Collation. a–d⁸, e⁴, f⁸ ; 44 leaves. 31 lines. With headlines and numbers to pages.

Leaf 1ᵃ Title, 1ᵇ blank, 2 Letter of C. Stephanus, 3ᵃ–36ᵇ Text, 37ᵃ–44ᵇ Indices. [*R.L.*] **[419¹.]**

BAIF (LAZARE DE). De re Vestiaria Libellus.
8°. *Haeredes S. Vincentii. Lyons*, 1536.
Title. DE RE VE- | STIARIA LIBEL- | LVS EX BAYFIO | EXCERPTVS | * | Addita uulgaris linguæ interpretatione, in adulescentulorum gratiam atq̃ utilitatem. | [Device] | LVGDVNI | APVD HÆREDES SIMONIS | VINCENTII | M.D. XXXVI. Leaf 36ᵃ *Colophon.* EXCVDEBANT LVGDVNI | MELCHIOR ET GASPAR | TRECHSEL FRATRES. | M.D.XXXVI.

Collation. a–d⁸, e⁴; 36 leaves. 29 lines. No headlines; with numbers to pages.

Leaf 1ᵃ Title, 1ᵇ Letter of C. Stephanus, 2ᵃ–31ᵇ Text, 32ᵃ–36ᵃ Indices, 36ᵇ blank. [*R.L.*] **[419².]**

—— De re Vestiaria. 8°. *Charles Estienne. Paris*, 1553.
Title. De re vestiaria, | Vascularia & Nauali : | Ex Bayfio. | In adolescentulorum, bonarum lite- | rarum studiosorum, gratiam. | [Device]. LVTETIAE, | Apud Carolum Stephanum, Typogra- | phum Regium. | M.D.LIII.

Collation. a–n⁸, o⁴ ; 108 leaves. 31 lines. With headlines and numbers to pages.

Leaf 1ᵃ Title, 1ᵇ blank, 2 Preface of C. Stephanus, 3ᵃ–95ᵃ Text, 95ᵇ–108ᵃ Index, 108ᵇ blank. [*R.L.*] **[716¹.]**

—— De Vasculis Libellus. 8°. *Haeredes S. Vincentii. Lyons*, 1536.
Title. DE VASCV | LIS LIBELLVS, ADV- | LESCENTVLORVM CAV- | sa ex Bayfio decerptus, | addita uulgari Lati- | narum uocum | interpreta- | tione. | [Device] | LVGDVNI, | APVD HÆREDES SIMONIS | VINCENTII | M.D.XXXVI. Leaf 28ᵇ *Colophon.*

C 2

EXCVDEBANT LVGDV | NI MELCHIOR ET | GASPAR TRECHSEL | FRATRES. 1536.

Collation. a, c⁸, d⁴; 28 leaves. 31 lines. No headlines; with numbers to pages.

Leaf 1ᵃ Title, 1ᵇ blank, 2 Letter of C. Stephanus, 3ᵃ–25ᵇ Text, 26ᵃ–28ᵇ Indices. [*R. T.*]   [419⁴.]

BALE (JOHN).   Apology against a rank papist.
                                      8°. *John Day.   London* [1555.]
Title. The Apology | of Iohan Bale agaynste | a ranke Papyst, aunswer-ing both | hym and hys doctours, that neyther their | vowes nor yet their priesthode are of the | Gospell, but of Antichrist. Anno | Do. M.CCCCC.L. | [*etc.*]   Leaf 160ᵃ *Colophon.* ⊄ Imprinted | at London by Ihon | Day, dwelling ouer Al- | dersgate.   These bokes are | to be sold at his shop, by | the lytle Conduit | in Chepe | syde. | ⊄ Cum priuilegio ad impri- | mendum solum.   Leaf 160ᵇ. ⊄ A dyspatche of vowes | and presthode, by the wurd | of God.   Compyled by | Iohan Bale.

Collation. A–V⁸; 160 leaves. 30 lines. With headlines and numbers to pages.

Leaf 1ᵃ Title, 1ᵇ blank, 2ᵃ–7ᵃ Bale's dedication to Edward VI, 7ᵇ–15ᵃ Preface, 15ᵇ–157ᵃ Text, 157ᵇ–159ᵇ Table, 160ᵃ Colophon, 160ᵇ "A dyspatche." [*B.L.*]   [108².]

BARNES (ROBERT).   A supplication unto Henry VIII.
                                    4to. *John Byddell.   London,* 1534.

Begins on B 1.   A supplicacion vnto the most gracious prynce H. the viii.

Leaf 78ᵇ *Colophon.* ⊄ Imprinted at London in Fletestrete by Johñ Byddell | at the signe of our lady of Pitie, nexte to Flete | brydge.   The yere of our lorde God | .1534. in the moneth of | Nouember.

B–V⁴, X²; 78 leaves. 43, 44 lines. With headlines; no numbers to pages. [*B.L.*]   [958².]

All copies of this book that are known want the first quire, which may have been suppressed or perhaps never printed.   On the verso of Q 1 is a small portrait presumed to be that of Barnes.

BARTHOLOMAEUS ANGLICUS.   De proprietatibus rerum.
fol.   *Wynkyn de Worde.*   *Westminster* [1495.]

Title.   Bartholomeu^s de | proprietatib$_3$ re$\,\text{ų}$ | Ends leaf 477^b.   ⊄ Ye that be nobly groundid all in grace | Experte in wysdom and philosophy | To you this processe comyth a myghty pace | whyche I dyrect to you that perfytlye | Ye may reforme to voyde all vylenye | Of euery thyng yf ought be here amysse | Excusyng theym whiche ment ryght well in this.   Leaf 478^a Caxton's device.   Leaf 478^b Bartholomeu^s de | proprietatib$_3$ re$\,\text{ų}$.

Collation.   a^6, B^8, b^6, c–z^8, &^{6}, ℈^{8}, A–V^8, X–Z^6, aa–cc^8, dd–gg^6, hh–mm^8, nn^4, oo^6; 478 leaves.   42 lines.   With headlines; no numbers to pages.

Leaf 1^a Title, 1^b Verses, 2 Prologue, 3^a–5^b Bk. 1, 6 blank, 7^a–202^a Books 2–11, 202^b blank, 203^a–475^b Books 12–19, 476^a–477^b List of authors and epilogue, 478^a Caxton's device, 478^b Title repeated.   [*B.L.*]
[2126.]

This copy wants leaves 1–4, 6, 478.   The preliminary leaves have been supplied in manuscript.

The title, which is repeated on the last leaf, is printed from a wood-block with white letters on a black ground.   There are numerous illustrations in the text.   In the epilogue the printer's name is given and Caxton is spoken of as printing the Latin edition at Cologne.   It is also stated that the book is printed on paper made in England by John Tate.

BERNERS (JULIANA).   The books of hawking, hunting, and coat armour.   fol.   *St. Alban's,* 1486.

Leaf 2^a.   IN so moch that gentill men and honest persones haue gre- | ete delite in haukyng and desire to haue the maner to take | haukys : and also how and in waat wyse they shulde gyde theym | ordynateli, [*etc.*] Leaf 89^b *Colophon.*   ⊄ Here in thys boke afore ar contenyt the bokys of haukyng | and huntyng with other plesuris dyuerse as in the boke apperis | and also of Cootarmuris a nobull werke.   And here now en- | dyth the boke of blasyng of armys translatyt and compylyt to | gedyr at Seynt albons the yere from thincarnacion of owre | lorde Ihū Crist. M.CCCC.lxxxvi. Leaf 90^a [Device of printer]   ⊄ Sanctus albanus :

Collation.   a–c^8, d^4, e, f^8, a b^6, c–e^8, f^{10}; 90 leaves.   32 lines.   Without headlines or numbers to pages.

Leaf 1 blank, 2^a–28^a Book of Hawking, 28^b blank, 29^a–44^a Book of Hunting, 44^b blank, 45^a–55^b Book of Coat-armour, 56 blank, 57^a–89^b Blasyng of arms, 90^a device and imprint, 90^b blank.   [1985.]

Wants leaves 1, 29–44 (The Book of Hunting), 72, 90.

BERNERS (JULIANA). The books of hawking, hunting and coat armour. fol. *Wynkyn de Worde. Westminster,* 1496.

Leaf 1ᵇ. ℂ This present boke shewyth the manere of hawkynge &⁓ hun- | tynge : and also of diuysyng of Cote armours It shewyth also | a good matetere [*sic*] belongynge to horses : wyth other cōmendable | treatyses. And ferdermore of the blasynge of armys : as here af | ter it maye appere. Leaf 73ᵇ *Colophon.* Enprynted at Westmestre by wynkyn de worde the | yere of thyncarnacōn of our lorde.M.CCCC.lxxxxvi.

Collation. a–e⁶, f, g⁴, h⁶, i⁴; a–c⁶, d⁸; 74 leaves. Without headlines or numbers to pages.

Leaf 1ᵃ Woodcut, 1ᵇ Woodcut and title, 2ᵃ–37ᵃ Book of Hawking and hunting, 37ᵇ–48ᵇ Book of Fishing, 49ᵃ–73ᵇ Book of blasyng of arms, 74ᵃ Woodcut, 74ᵇ Caxton's device. [*B.L.*] **[1984.]**

Wants last leaf.

BIBLE (*Latin*). Biblia, interprete Sebastiano Castalione.
fol. *J. Oporinus. Basileae,* 1551

Title. BIBLIA | Interprete Sebastiano | Castalione. | VNA CVM EIVSDEM | Annotationibus. | . . . BASILEAE, PER IO- | annem Oporinum. | Leaf 424ᵃ *Colophon.* BASILEAE, PER IACOBVM | Parcum, sumptibus Ioannis Oporini. Anno | Salutis humanæ M.D.LI. | Mense Martio.

Collation. &⁓, A–Z⁶, &⁓⁸, AA–ZZ, &⁓&⁓, AAA–LLL⁶, MMM⁴, NNN⁶, aaaa–hhhh⁶, iiii⁴; 424 leaves, 57 lines. With headlines and numbers to pages.

Leaf 1ᵃ *Title,* 1ᵇ blank, 2ᵃ–5ᵃ Dedication to Edward VI, 5ᵇ–6ᵃ Ad lectores, 6ᵇ Order of books, 7ᵃ–152ᵃ Genesis to Esther, 152ᵇ blank, 153ᵃ–296ᵃ Job to Maccabees, 296ᵇ blank, 297ᵃ Title to N.T., 297ᵇ blank, 298ᵃ–371ᵃ New Testament, 371ᵇ 372 blank, 373ᵃ–423ᵇ Annotationes, 424ᵃ Register and colophon, 424ᵇ blank. [*R.L.*] **[2273.**

Contains autographs " Worthington " " Willm Worthington Junior."

—— The Bible in English. fol. *R. Grafton and E. Whitchurch.* 1539.

Title [within border]. ℂ The Byble in | Englysshe, that is to saye the con- | tent of all the holy scrypture, bothe | of yᵉ olde and newe testament truly | translated after the veryte of the | Hebrue and Greke textes, by yᵉ dy- | lygent studye of dyuerse excellent | learned men, expert in the for sayde | tonges. | ℂ Prynted by Rychard Grafton &⁓ | Edward Whitchurch. |

Cum priuilegio ad imprimen- | dum solum. | 1539. | Leaf 530^b *Colophon.*
The ende of the new Testamēt : | and of the whole Byble, Fynisshed in
Apryll, | Anno. M.CCCCC.XXXIX. | + | A dño factū est istud.

Collation. *⁶, a–k⁸, l⁴, A–P⁸, Q⁴, AA–PP⁸, QQ, RR, ⁶ ; Aaa–Kkk⁸,
Aa–Nn⁸ ; 530 leaves, 62 lines. With headlines and numbers to pages.

Leaf 1^a Title, 1^b List of books, 2^a–3^b Kalendar and Almanach, 4^a–5^a
Exhortation, 5^b Prologue, 6 List of Kings, 7^a–90^a Genesis to Deuteronomy,
90^b blank, 91^a Second title, 91^b blank, 92^a–213^b Joshua to Job, 214 blank,
215^a Third Title, 215^b blank, 216^a–346^a Psalms to Malachi, 346^b blank,
347^a Fourth Title, 347^b To the reader, 348^a–426^b Esdras to Maccabees,
427^a Title to N.T., 427^b blank, 428^a–529^a New Testament, 529^a–530^b
Table. [*B.L.*]   [**2638.**]

This copy, which is in poor condition in parts, wants leaves 214 (a blank)
and 507–514 (sig. Ll.).

This is the first edition of the " Great " or " Cromwell's " Bible. The
printing was commenced under the superintendence of Coverdale and
Grafton by Francis Regnault at Paris in 1538. In December the
Inquisitor-general of France put a stop to the printing, but most of what
had already been finished was safely transferred to England. Type and
workmen were procured from France and the book finished in April, 1539.
The only copy known printed on vellum, the presentation copy to
Cromwell, is now in the library of St. John's College, Cambridge.

Westcott, Hist. of the English Bible, pp. 73–83.

BIBLE.   Old Testament.   [Psalms.]   Certain psalms.
        8°.   *Thomas Raynald and John Harryngton. London,* 1549.

Title. Certayne psal- | mes chosen out of the psal- | ter of Dauid,
commonlye | called thee VII. penytentiall psal- | mes, drawen into englyshe
me- | ter by Sir Thomas Wyat | Knyght, wherunto is ad- | ded a prologe
of yᵉ auc- | tore before euery psal- | me, very pleasaūt &ᵛ | profettable to
the | godly reader. | ☙ Imprinted | at London in Paules | Churchyarde,
at the sygne | of thee Starre, By | Thomas Ray- | nald. | and John
Harryngton | Leaf 36^a *Colophon.* ◖| Cum Preuilegio ad imprimendum |
Solum, | MD.XLIX. The last | day of December.

Collation. A–D⁸, E⁴ ; 36 leaves. 24 lines. No headlines or numbers
to pages.

Leaf 1^a Title, 1^b–2^b Haryngton's letter to the Marquis of Northhampton,
3^a–6^a Prologue of the author, 6^a–36^a text, 36^b blank. [*B.L.*]   [**75³.**]

BIBLE.   Old Testament. [Appendix.]   The images of the Old Testament.
4to. *Jean Frellon.   Lyons*, 1549.

Title. THE | IMAGES | OF THE OLD | TESTAMENT, | Lately expressed, set forthe in Ynglishe and | Frenche, vuith a playn and | brief exposition. | [Device] | Printed at Lyons, by Iohan Frellon, the | yere of lord God, 1549.

Collation. [2] B–M⁴, N²; 48 leaves.   No headlines or numbers to pages.

Leaf 1ᵃ Title, 1ᵇ Epistle of Franciscus Frellonius, 2ᵃ–47ᵇ Text, 48ᵃ Device, 48ᵇ blank. [*R.L.*]   [**946.**]

The woodcuts are from designs by Hans Holbein.

—— New Testament.   Latin and English.
4to. *James Nicholson.   London*, 1538.

Title [within borders].   The newe tes- | tament both Latine and | Englyshe ech correspondente to | the other after the vulgare texte, com- | munely called S. Jeromes. Fayth- | fully translated [by Myles | Couerdale] | Anno. M.CCCCC.XXXVIII. | Jeremie. XXII. | Is not my worde lyke a fyre sayeth the | LORDE, and lyke an hammer that | breaketh the harde stone ? | Printed in Southwarke | by James Nicolson. | Set forth wyth the kyn- | ges moost gracious licence.   Ends leaf 348ᵇ.   ℭ The ende of the new | Testament. | ℭ Finis noui testamenti.

Collation. [+⁶], A–Z, Aa–VV⁸; 350 leaves.   41 lines.   With headlines and numbers to pages.

Leaf 1ᵃ Title, 1ᵇ blank, 2ᵃ–3ᵃ Dedication, 3ᵇ–4ᵇ To the reader, 5, 6 Almanack, 7ᵃ–348 Text, 349, 350 Table of Epistles and gospels. [*B.L.*]   [**1277.**]

This copy wants leaves 2, 3, 4, 349, 350.   The words given in brackets have been erased from the title-page.

—— The New Testament.   4to. *Richard Jugge.   London* [1552.]

Title. ℛ The newe Testament | of our Sauiour Jesu Christe.   Faythfully tran- | slated out of the Greke. | ℭ Wyth the Notes and expositions of the darke pla- | ces therein. | Viuat [Portrait of Edward VI] Rex. | Mathew. xiii. f. | Vnio, quem præcepit emi seruator Iesus, | Hic situs est, debet non aliunde peti. | The pearle, which Christ cõmaunded to be bought | Is here to be founde, not elles to be sought.   Leaf 339ᵇ *Colophon.*   [Printer's device] Imprynted at London by Rycharde Jugge, dwel- | lynge in Paules churche yarde at the signe of the byble. | VVith the kynge his mooste gratious lycence, and | priuilege, forbyddynge all other men to print | or cause to be printed, this, or any other | Testament in Englyshe.

Collation. *, ♨, A–Z⁸, & ⁴, Aa–Rr⁸ ; 340 leaves. 37 lines. With headlines ; no numbers to pages.

Leaf 1ᵃ Title, 1ᵇ blank, 2 Dedication, 3ᵃ–8ᵇ Kalendar, 9ᵃ Almanack, 9ᵇ–14ᵇ Table, 15 Computation of years, 16ᵃ Exhortation, 16ᵇ Life of Matthew, 17ᵃ–204ᵃ Text, 204ᵇ colophon. 205ᵃ Title, 205ᵇ–339ᵃ Text, 339ᵇ Colophon, 340 blank. [*B.L.*] **[1671.]**

Though this edition is without date there is no doubt that it was issued during the first half of 1552. In some copies an authorisation of the Privy Council is printed on the reverse of the title-page, which fixes the price at not more than 22 pence (about a farthing a sheet) and this is dated 10 June, 1552. Again in the tables reference is made to a second communion on Easter Day, omitted from the service books in August, 1552.

LE BLAZON DES ARMES. 8°. *Philippe le Noir. Paris* [1530.]

Title. Le blazon des ar | mes : auec les armes des Princes & Sei- | gneurs de France. | [Woodcut of arms.] Leaf 23ᵃ *Colophon.* ¶ Cy finist le blason des armes. | Imprime a paris en la grant rue | saint iaques par phelipe le noir.

Collation. A–G⁴ ; 28 leaves. 23 lines. No headlines or numbers to pages.

Leaf 1ᵃ Title, 1ᵇ Cut of arms, 2ᵃ–23ᵃ Text, 23ᵇ, 24ᵃ blank, 24ᵇ–27ᵇ Arms of kings, 28ᵃ blank, 28ᵇ Device of P. le Noir. [*B.L.*] **[46².]**

By Sicille, Herald to Alphonso V, King of Aragon. A number of editions are mentioned by Brunet, but this is not amongst them.

BOECE (HECTOR). The history and chronicles of Scotland.

fol. *Thomas Davidson. Edinburgh* [1540.]

Title. ♋ Heir beginnis the hystory and | croniklis of Scotland ∴ | [Woodcut]. Leaf 286ᵃ *Colophon.* ♋ Heir endis the hystory and | Croniklis of Scotland, with the Cosmography & dyscription thairof, | Compilit be the noble clerk maister Hector Boece channon of Aber- | dene. Translatit laitly in our vulgar and commoun langage, be | maister Johne Bellenden Archedene of Murray, And Im- | prentit in Edinburgh, be me Thomas Dauidson, | prenter to the kyngis nobyll grace ∴ | ☞ CVM PRIVILEGIO ✿.

Collation.   A–F⁶, A–Y⁶ᐟ⁴, Z⁶, Aa⁴, Bb–Gg⁶ᐟ⁴, Hh⁶, Ii¹⁰, Kk⁴, Ll–Yy⁶ᐟ⁴, Zz, &ᐟ&ᐟ⁶, ꝏ⁸ ; 286 leaves.   47 lines.   With headlines and numbers to pages.

Leaf 1ᵃ Title, 1ᵇ Excusation of printer, 2ᵃ Contents, 2ᵇ–6ᵃ Proheme of the Cosmography, 6ᵇ–21ᵇ Cosmography, 22ᵃ–31ᵇ Table, 32ᵃ–33ᵃ List of Kings, 33ᵇ blank, 34ᵃ–36ᵇ Proheme of the History, 37ᵃ–286ᵃ Text, 286ᵇ Woodcut.   [*B.L.*]   [2071.]

On the title-page is a large woodcut of the arms of Scotland, and on the last page a cut of the Crucifixion with a background of saints within a large floral circle.   Two small woodcuts in the text depict a fight between some knights, and a Crucifixion.

Various dates have been assigned to this book, the most generally accepted being 1542.   However a copy was lately noticed in the Innerpeffray library containing a note stating that it was given to the library by Alexander Dick, Archdeacon of Glasgow in 1540.   Thomas Davidson the printer is only known to have printed three other books. Of the Chronicles several copies printed on vellum are known, one in the Edinburgh University Library, another at Ham House, and the finest in the collection of J. Pierpont Morgan.

BONAVENTURA.   Speculum vitae Christi.
                          fol.   *Richard Pynson.*   [*London.*] [1506.]

Leaf 1 begins ☾ Incipit speculum vite xpi. | AT the begynnynge of this phemy of the boke that is clepyd | the myrrour of the blessyd lyfe of iesu cryst.   The first part for | the monday. a deuoute medytacyon of the greate counsell in | heuen for the restorynge of man and his saluacyon.   Capitulū primū. | [*etc.*].   Ends leaf 100ᵃ.   ☾ In omni tribulatione temptacione, necessitate et angustia : succurre | nobis piissima virgo maria.   Amen. | ☾ Emprynted by Rychard Pynson.

Collation.   A–O⁶, P, Q⁸ ; 100 leaves.   44 lines.   With headlines ; no numbers to pages.

Leaf 1ᵃ–2ᵃ Table, 2ᵇ–4ᵇ Prohemium, 5ᵃ–100ᵃ Text, 100ᵇ Pynson's device 3.   [*B.L.*]   [2051³.]

With woodcuts.   The only copy known of this edition.

The date can be fairly accurately settled from the state of the device.

An old manuscript inscription runs "Robard Spencer lederseller of london aremit of the chappell of sant katheryn at charyng crosse."

BONAVENTURA. Speculum vite Christi.

4to. *Wynkyn de Worde. London,* 1530.

Title. ⁋ Uita Christi. Leaf 167ᵇ *Colophon.* ⁋ Thus endeth the lyfe of our lorde Iesu Chryst, af- | ter Bonauenture. Imprynted at London in Flete | strete at the sygne of the sonne, by me Wynkyn de | Worde. The yere of our lorde god . M.CCCCC | XXX . and fynysshed the . viij . daye of February.

Collation. . A⁶, B⁸, C⁴, D⁸, E–M⁴/⁵, N⁸, O⁸, P–Y⁴/⁸, Z⁴, AA⁸, BB⁴, CC⁸, DD⁶ ; 168 leaves. 32 lines. With headlines ; no numbers to pages.

Leaf 1ᵃ Title, 1ᵇ–3ᵇ Table, 4ᵃ–8ᵇ Prohemium, 9ᵃ–167ᵇ Text, 168ᵃ Woodcut, 168ᵇ W. de Worde's device 12. [*B.L.*]   [1011².]

With woodcuts. Wants last leaf.

BONNER (EDMUND). A profitable and necessary doctrine.

4to. *John Cawood. London,* 1555.

Title [within a border]. ⁋ A profita | ble and necessarye do- | ctryne, with certayne ho- | melies adioyned thervnto | set forth by the reuerende | father in God, Edmonde | byshop of London, for the | instruction and enformati- | on of the people beynge | within his Diocesse of | London, & of his cure | and charge. | Declina a malo, & fac bonum. | Presis, vt prosis. Leaf 203ᵃ *Colophon.* ⧯ EXCVSVM | LONDINI IN ÆDIBVS IO- | hannis Cawodi, Typographi Regiæ | Maiestatis. | Anno. 1555, Mensis Septembris. 17.

Collation. A–Z, &, Aa–Zz, &&, Aaa–Ccc⁴ [4]; 206 leaves. 31 lines. With headlines ; no numbers to pages.

Leaf 1ᵃ Title, 1ᵇ blank, 2ᵃ–4ᵃ Preface, 4ᵇ blank, 5ᵃ–203ᵃ Text, 203ᵇ–206ᵃ Faults escaped. 206ᵇ blank. [*B.L.*]   [1257¹.]

Leaf 202 cancelled.

——— Homelies.

4to. *John Cawood. London,* 1555.

Title. [Within a border.] HOME- | lies sette forth by the | righte reuerende father in | God, Edmunde Byshop of | London, not onely promi- | sed before in his booke, inti- | tuled, A necessary doctrine, | but also now of late adioy- | ned, and added therevnto, | to be read within his dio- | cesse of London, of all per- | sons, vycars, and curates, | vnto theyr parishioners, v- | pon sondayes, & holydayes. | Anno. M.D.LV.

Leaf 74ᵃ *Colophon.* ꗃ Imprinted at Lon | don in Poules churcheyarde, at the sygne of | the holy Ghost, by Iohn Cawodde, Pryn- | ter to the kynge and Queenes | Maiesties. | Cum priuilegio Regiæ maiestatis.

Collation.   A–S⁴, T² ;   74 leaves.   31 lines.   With headlines and numbers to pages.

Leaf 1ᵃ Title, 1ᵇ Table, 2ᵃ Address of the Bishop, 2ᵇ–73ᵇ Text, 74ᵃ colophon, 74ᵇ blank. [*B.L.*]   [1257².]

THE BOOK OF WISDOM.   8⁰.   *Robert Wyer.   London,* 1532.

Title.   ꗃ The boke of | wysdome, folowynge the aucto- | ryties of auncyent Phylosophers, | Dyuydynge, and spekyng of vy | ces and vertues, wherby a | man maye be praysed, or | dyspraysed, with the | maner to speke al- | wayes well and | wysely to all folkes, | of what estate so | euer they be. | [Woodcut.]   Ends leaf 72ᵇ *Colophon.*   ꗃ Impzynted by me Robert wyer, | dwellynge at the sygne of saynt | Iohn̄ Euangelyste, in saynt | Martyns parysshe besyde | Charynge crosse.   The | yere of our Lorde god | M.CCCCC. and | xxxii. the .xx. day | of Ianuarii. | ꗃ Cum priuilegio Regali : pro | spatio septem annorum.

Collation.   a–s⁴ ;   72 leaves.   27 lines.   With headlines and numbers to pages.

Leaf 1ᵃ Title, 1ᵇ–2ᵇ Prologue, 3ᵃ–68ᵇ Text, 69ᵃ–72ᵇ Table and colophon. [*B.L.*]   [19².]

This work is apparently a translation [by J Larke ?] from a French version of the Italian Fiore di Virtu.

Herbert I, p. 369.   Plomer No. 3.

BORDE (ANDREW).   The introduction of knowledge.
                          4⁰.   *William Copland.   London* [1548.]
Title.   ꗃ The fyrst boke of the | Introduction of knowledge.   The whych | dothe teache a man to speake parte of all maner of | languages, and to know the vsage and fashion of | all maner of countreys.   And for to know the | moste parte of all maner of coynes of mo- | ney, the whych is currant in euery region | Made by Andrew Borde, of Phy- | sycke Doctor. Dedycated to | the right honorable & gra- | ciō̄ lady Mary dough- | ter of our souerayne | Lorde king Henry | the eyght. | + | [Woodcut.]   Leaf 52ᵇ *Colophon.*   ꗃ Imprinted at Lon- | don in Fleetestrete, at the Signe | of the Rose Garland, by me | william Copland. | (.˙.) | [Device.]

Collation. A–N⁴; 52 leaves.   33 lines.   No headlines or numbers to pages.

Leaf 1ᵃ Title, 1ᵇ Dedication, 1ᵇ–3ᵃ Table, 3ᵇ–52ᵃ Text, 52ᵇ Colophon. [*B.L.*]   [**843.**]

This is the first edition of which one other copy is known, now in the library of Britwell Court.

With numerous woodcuts, for the most part used previously by other printers.

This book was commenced by Robert Copland, and is referred to several times by Borde in his other works. In the Breviary of Health he writes of his "Introduction of Knowledge whiche hath bene longe a pryntynge, for lacke of money and paper, and it is in pryntynge, with pyctures, at Roberte Coplande, prynter."

BUDÉ (GUILLAUME).   Lucubrationes.

                    fol.   *Nicolaus Episcopius.*   *Basle,* 1557.

Title.   GVLIELMI BVDAEI | PARISIENSIS, CONSILIARII RE- | GII, SVPPLICVMQVE LIBELLORVM IN REGIA MAGI- | stri, Lucubrationes uarie, cum ad studiorum rectam institutionem ac Phi- | lologiam, tum ad pietatem spectantes: quibus adiunximus Epistola- | rum | eiusdem Latinarum ac Graecarum libros VI. non omissis etiam iis | quæ ex Græcis in Latinam linguam conuertit: quo- | rum nomenclaturam uersa facie uidebis. | INDEX OMNIVM IN HISCE MEMORA- | bilium rerum ac uocum his additus est. | [Device of Episcopius] Τῆς 'επιμλείας δυλα παντα γίνεται. | BASILEAE APVD NICOLAVM EPISCO- | pium Iuniorem. M.D.LVII.   Leaf 293ᵇ *Colophon.*   BASILEAE, APUD NICOLAVM EPISCOPIVM | IVNIOREM, ANNO M.D.LVII. | MENSE SEPTEMBRI.

Collation.   Aa⁴, BB–DD⁶, a–z, A–X⁶, Y⁸; 294 leaves.   54 lines.   With headlines and numbers to pages.

Leaf 1ᵃ Title, 1ᵇ catalogue of works, 2ᵃ–4ᵇ Coelius Secundus Curio to Joannes Fichardus, 5ᵃ–22ᵃ Index, 22ᵇ blank, 23ᵃ–293ᵇ text, 294ᵃ blank, 294ᵇ Printer's device.   [**2343.**]

CARDANUS (HIERONYMUS).   De libris propriis.

                  8°.   *Gulielmus Rovillius.*   *Lyons,* 1557.

Title.   HIERONYMI | CARDANI ME- | DIOLANENSIS | MEDICI LIBER | DE LIBRIS | PROPRIIS. | [Device.] | LVGDVNI, | Apud Gulielmum Rouillium, | sub scuto Veneto. | 1557. | Cum Priuilegio Regis.

Collation. a–m⁸, n⁴ ; 100 leaves. 27 lines. No headlines ; with numbers to pages.

Leaf 1ᵃ Title, 1ᵇ blank, 2ᵃ–7ᵇ Letter of Cardanus to N. Siccus, 7ᵇ–99ᵇ text, 100 blank. [*R.L.*] [716².]

CARMELIANUS (PETRUS). Foedus matrimonii.

4to. *Richard Pynson. London,* [1508].

Leaf 1ᵃ. ℂ Petri Carmeliani Carmen. Anglia per petuos : tibi dar [*sic*] rosa rubra triūphos [*etc.*, 8 lines]. Below this royal arms crowned and supported by angels [53 × 76]: and below this crowned rose and crowned portcullis [53 × 34]. Border as on other pages. Leaf 1ᵇ begins. Hoc presenti libello humili stilo edi- | to ad facmorem legētiū intellectū | Cōtinentur honoritica gesta So- | lemnes cerimonie & triūphi nuper habiti | In sus-cipiēda magna atq̄ egregia sacra- | tissimi prīcipis Maximiliani Romanoꝛ | Imperatoris, semper augusti, Simul et | Illustrissimi ac potētessimi sui filu Karoli | Principis castelle Archiducis austrie Le- | gatione. Ad serenissimū potētissimumq̄ | principē Hēricū septimū Anglie & Frācie | Regem, dñmq̄ hybernie, destinata. Pro | spōsalibus et matrimonio Inter prefatū | Illustrissimū principem Karolum, & illu- | strissimū ac nobilissimā prīcipem Domi- | nam Mariam prenominati regis Hērici | filiā charissimam Cōtrahendis. Necnon | Ritus & ordo in huiusmodi sponsalioꝛ et | matrimonii celebratione adhibiti & obser | uati. . . . [&c.]

Collation. A⁶, B⁴, C⁶, D E⁴ ; 24 leaves, 24 lines. No headlines or numbers to pages.

Leaf 1ᵃ Title, 1ᵇ–23ᵇ Text, 24ᵃ Verses, 24ᵇ Pynson's device. *B.L.* [945.]

Each page is surrounded with a border, and there are full page woodcuts on 7ᵃ and 14ᵇ of the reception of the ambassadors and the formal betrothal.

The first and last leaves are much mutilated. The title and beginning given above are taken from a copy (on vellum) in the British Museum, G. 6118.

CESSOLIS (JACOBUS DE). The Game of Chess.

fol. *William Caxton.* [*Westminster.*] [1483.]

Leaf 2ᵃ. tHe holy appostle and doctour of the peple saynt | Poule sayth in his epystle. Alle that is wryten | is wryten vnto our doctryne and for our ler-|nyng. Wherfore many noble clerkes haue endeuoyred | [*etc.*]. Leaf 84ᵃ, line 25. man but as a beste. Thenne late euery man of what | condycion he be that redyth or herith this litel book redde. | take therby ensaumple to amende hym. | Explicit per Caxton.

Collation. a–i⁸, k, l⁶ ; 84 leaves.   29 lines.   No headlines or numbers to pages.

Leaf 1 blank, 2ᵃ–2ᵇ Preface, 2ᵇ–3ᵃ Table of chapters, 3ᵇ blank, 4ᵃ–84ᵃ Text, 84ᵇ blank. [*B.L.*]   **[1945.]**

Contains sixteen different woodcuts, many of which are used twice.

Wants leaf 1.   Leaf 84 almost all wanting.

CHASTISING OF GOD'S CHILDREN.

fol. [Wynkyn de Worde. Westminster, 1492.]

Title. ℂ The prouffytable boke for mañes soule, And right comfor- | table to the body, and specyally in aduersitee &ᵛ trybulacyon, whiche | boke is called The Chastysing of goddes Chyldern.   Leaf 48ᵃ, col. 2, line 24. brynge from all manere dysease in | to ful Joye &ᵛ blisse, Now god gra | unt that it myghte so be that euer | is lastyng in Trinyte.

Collation. [2] A–G⁶, H⁴ ; 48 leaves.   36 lines.   Without headlines or numbers to pages.

Leaf 1ᵃ Title, 1ᵇ Preface, 2 Table, 3ᵃ–48ᵃ Text, 48ᵇ blank.   [*B.L.*]
[2051¹.]

CHAUCER (GEOFFREY).   The Canterbury Tales.

fol. [William Caxton. Westminster, 1484.]

Leaf 2ᵃ.   Prohemye | gRete thankes lawde and honour, ought to be gy | ven vnto the clerkes, poetes, and historiographs | that haue wreton many noble bokes of wysedom, [*etc.*].   Leaf 312ᵃ, line 5. be one of hem at the day of dome that shal be sauyd, Qui cum | patre et spiritu sancto viuit et regnat deus. Per omnia secula | seculorum AMEN,

Collation. a–t⁸, v⁶, aa–hh⁸, ii⁶, A–K⁸, L⁴ ; 312 leaves.   38 lines.   With headlines ; no numbers to pages.

Leaf 1 blank, 2ᵃ Caxton's prologue, 3ᵃ–312ᵃ Text, 312ᵇ blank.   [*B.L.*]
Wants four leaves.   **[2053.]**

CHRISTINE DE PISAN.   The fayts of arms and of chivalry.

fol. William Caxton. [Westminster.] 1489.

Leaf 1ᵃ.   HEre begynneth the table of the rubryshys of the | boke of the fayt of armes and of Chyualrye whiche | sayd boke is departyd in to foure partyes, [*etc.*].   Leaf 3ᵃ.   Here begynneth the book of fayttes of armes &ᵛ of Chyual- | rye, And the first chapytre is the prologue, in which xpry- | styne of pyse excuseth hir self to haue dar enterpryse to speke | of so hye matere as is conteyned in this sayd book | [*etc.*].   Leaf 143ᵇ,

line 26. present lyf, that after thys short & transitorye lyf, he may at- |
teyne to euerlastpng [*sic*] lyf in heuen, Whiche god gaunte [*sic*] to | hym
and to alle his lyege peple AMEN, | Per Caxton.

Collation. [2] A–R⁸, S⁶ ; 144 leaves. 31 lines. No headlines or
numbers to pages.

Leaf 1–2ᵃ Table, 2ᵇ blank, 3ᵃ–143ᵇ Text. [*B.L.*]　　　　　　[1938¹.]
Wants last leaf.

CHRONICLES OF ENGLAND.　fol.　*W. Caxton. Westminster*, 1482.

Six leaves only. [*B.L.*]　　　　　　　　　　　　　　　　[1997¹.]

——　　　　　　　fol.　[*William de Machlinia. London*, 1485.]

Leaf 1ᵃ. Fyrst in the prologue is conceyued how Albyne wi | th his
susters entrid in to this Ile and named | yt Albyon　Leaf 11ᵃ. How the
lande of Englonde was fyrst namd Al | bion. And bi what encheson it
was so namd. Leaf 238ᵃ, line 32. in thise daies is sore mynushed by the
puissaūce of the tur | kes & hethē men & that aft⁷ this presēt & short
lyfe we may | cõ to the euerlasting lyfe in the blisse of heuen Amen.

Collation. a¹⁰, A–Z, &, aa–dd⁸, ee⁴ ; 238 leaves. 33 lines. Without
headlines or numbers to pages.

Leaf 1ᵃ–10ᵃ Table of contents, 10ᵇ blank, 11ᵃ–238ᵃ Text, 238ᵇ blank.
[*B.L.*]　　　　　　　　　　　　　　　　　　　　　　[1997².]
Very imperfect.

COLET (JOHN). Editio.　　　　　　　　8°. [*Antwerp.*] 1534.

Leaf 1ᵃ. ❧ IOANNIS | COLETI THEOLO- | gi, olim Decani Diui
Pauli, | æditio, vna cum quibusdam | G. Lilii Grammatices | Rudimentis. |
G. LILII EPIGRAMMA. | Pocula si linguæ cupias gustare Latinæ, |
Quale tibi monstret, ecce Coletus iter, | Non per caucaseos montes, aut
summa Pyrene, | Te ista per Hybleos sed uia ducit agros. | M.D.XXXIIII. |
Ends leaf 43ᵇ. ⊄ Hæc breuiter de syllabarum quantitate | dicta sufficiant.

Collation. B–F⁸, G⁴ ; 44 leaves. 28 lines. No headlines or numbers
to pages.

Leaf 1ᵃ Title, 1ᵇ Master to parents, 2ᵃ–5ᵇ Prayers and prologues,
5ᵇ–43ᵇ Text. [*R. & Ital. L.*]　　　　　　　　　　　　[424¹.]
Last leaf wanting.

The reason for this book beginning with signature B is that it was
customary to prefix to it Wolsey's exhortation to the masters of Ipswich
School, which usually consisted of one gathering. Bibliographica, I. p. 186.

COLET (JOHN). Paules Accidence.   8°. [*Antwerp.*] [1535.]

Title [within border]. ⧼ Paules Accidence | ✑ Johannis Coleti Theologi, | olim decani diui Pauli, æditio | vna cum quibusdam Guil. Lilii | Grammatices rudimentis. | ☞ Guil. Lilii Epigramma. | Pocula si linguæ cupias gusta- | re latinæ, | Quale tibi monstret, ecce | Coletus Iter. | Non per caucaseos montes, aut | summa Pyrines. | Te ista per Hybleos, seu uia ducit agros. Ends leaf 48ᵇ. And one nown in the datyue, as, He dwel | leth vplonde, or in the countre. Manet ruri. | FINIS.

Collation. A–Fˢ ; 48 leaves.

Leaf 1ᵃ Title, 1ᵇ–8ᵃ Prefatory matter and prayers, 8ᵃ–48ᵇ Text. [*R. & B.L.*] Bibliographica I. p. 185.   [424ˢ.]

CONSULADO DE MAR.   4to. *Francisco Diaz. Valencia,* 1539.

Title [within borders]. ⧼ Libro llamado Cōsulado | de mar. Obra muy vtil y prouechosa : y | aun muy necessaria : ansi para todo gene | ro de mercaderes : como de señores de | Naos : y pilotos : y marineros : y todos los que nauegā. [*etc.*]. ✑ Año de M.D.xxxviiij ✑ Leaf 166ᵃ *Colophon.* Haze fin | el presente libro : llamado Consulado | de mar. Agora nueuamente traduzi | do dⁿ lengua Catalana en nr̄o vul | gar Castellano. Ha sido im- | presso en la metropolitana | ciudad de Ualencia : | por Francisco Diaz | Romano. A. iiii. | dias del mes | de Enero. | Año de. | 1539. | +.

Collation. +, A–Tˢ, V⁶ ; 166 leaves. 36 lines. With headlines and numbers to pages.

Leaf 1ᵃ Title, 1ᵇ–8ᵇ Table, 9ᵃ–166ᵃ Text, 166ᵇ blank. [*B.L.*] [1577.]

This popular work on maritime law was first printed at Barcelona in 1494 and frequently reprinted in various versions later. Brunet II. 234.

LE GRAND COUTUMIER DE NORMANDIE.

fol. *L. Hostingue for M. Angier (Caen) and J. Mace (Rennes). Caen,* 1510.

Leaf 1ᵃ *Title.* Le grāt coustumier du pays & duche de nor | mendie tresutille & profitable a tous praticiens . . . . Nouuellement Imprime a Caen | par Laurens Hostingue demourant audit lieu deuant la | tour au Landoys. Pour Michel Angier Libraire & Relieur de | Luniuersite dud' Caen demourāt aud' lieu pres le pōt Sainct pierre | Et pour Jehan Mace aussi Libraire demourant a Renes en la paroisse | Saīct saulueur a lensigne saīt Jehā leuāgeliste. Et sōt a vendre ausd' lieux. | Et ont este acheuez Lan de grace Mil cinq cens et dix. Le. xxviii. iour Dapuril. | [*etc.*] Leaf 218ᵇ *Colophon.* ⧼ Cy finissent les ordonnances auec le grant coustumier

D

de Normādie et aussi la chartre | normande et autres ordōnances et editz faiz du Roy. Nouuellemēt Imprimees a Caen | pour Michiel angier demourant aud' lieu pres le pont Sainct pierre & Jehan mace de- | mourāt a Renes Et furēt acheuees le vingtsixiesme iour Dapuril. Mil Cinq centz et dix. | [Registrum].

Collation. a¹⁰, b–o⁸, pq⁶, A–E⁸, F¹⁰, G–I⁸, K¹⁰, mm⁶ ; 224 leaves.   45 or 63 lines.   With headlines and numbers to pages.

Leaf 1ᵃ Title, 1ᵇ Epistola, 2ᵃ–6ᵃ Repertoire, 6ᵇ–7ᵇ Prologue, 7ᵇ–134ᵇ Exposition, 135ᵃ–218ᵇ Jura et consuetudines, 219ᵃ–223ᵇ Arbor consanguinitatis, 224 blank.   Brunet II. 377.   [*B.L.*]   [1954.]

CRONICA CRONICARUM.

   fol. *Jaques Ferrebouc for Jean Petit and François Regnault. Paris,* 1521.

Leaf 1ᵇ begins : CRonica Cronicarum abbrege et mis par figures descentes | et Rondeaulx, cōtenans deux parties principalles, Dōt la premiere cōmēcāt a la creation du monde sera ordōnce & distincte par les cinq | aages iusques a laduenemēt de nostreseigneur Jesucrist. [*etc.*]. Leaf 32ᵃ *Colophon.* ℂ Imprime a Paris pour Jehan petit & Francoys regnault libraires | iurez d' luniuersite.   Et par Jaques ferrebouc Imprimeur le . xx . iour de | Septembre . Lan Mil cinq cens vingt et vng.

Collation.   A–P, a–r¹ ;   32 sheets.   102 lines.   [2992.]

Printed on single sheets on one side only in the manner of a broadside and intended to be either bound as a large volume by pasting the sheets back to back (as in the present instance), or made into a long roll by joining the sheets together at top and bottom.   Brunet I. 1861.

DIALOGUS.   Dyalogus creaturarum optime moralizatus.
                           fol.   *Gerard Leeu.   Gouda,* 1481.

Leaf 2ᵃ begins : [P]refacio in librum qui dicitur dyalogus creaturarum mo | ralizaℓ omni materie morali iocundo et edificatiuo mo- | do applicabilis Incipit feliciter.   Leaf 12ᵃ.   Dyalogus creaturarū optime moralizatus. omni materie morali io- | cūdo mō applicabilⁱᵒ : ad laudē dei & edificationē hoīm Incipit feliciter.   Leaf 104ᵃ.   Presens liber Dyalogus creaturarum appellatus iocundis fa | bulis plenus Per gerardum leeu in opido goudensi inceptus | munere dei finitus est Anno domini millesimo quadringente- | simo octuagesimo primo mensis iunij die sexta.

Collation.   [10] a–l⁸, m⁶ ;   104 leaves.   34 lines.   No headlines or numbers to pages.

Leaf 1 blank, 2 Prefatio, 3, 4 Prima Tabula, 5ᵃ–10ᵇ Secunda tabula, 11 blank, 12ᵃ–104ᵃ Text, 104ᵇ blank. [*G.L.*]   [2002².]

This copy wants leaf 1, and has the signatures k and l bound in the wrong order.

This work, profusely illustrated with a series of 121 woodcuts, rapidly became popular, and no less than six editions were issued at Gouda by G. Leeu between June, 1480, and August, 1482, the present copy belonging to the third.

Hain, 6125. Campbell, Annales, 561. Proctor, 8924.

DIALOGUES OF CREATURES MORALISED.
4to.   [*Martin de Keyser.*]   [*Antwerp.*] [1535.]

Title. ☞ The Dialoges of | Creatures Moralysed. Applyably and edificatyfly, | to euery mery and iocounde mater, of late trāslated out | of latyn into our Englysshe tonge right pro- | fitable to the gouernaunce of man. | ◖ And they be to sell, vpō | Powlys churche | yarde. | [Woodcut.] Leaf 163ᵇ *Colophon.* ◖ Thus endith the Dialogus of | Creatures Moralysed. Applyably and edificatyfly, | to euery mery and iocounde mater, of late trāslated out | of latyn into our Englysshe tonge right pro- | fitable to the gouernaunce of man. | ◖ And they be to sell, vpō | Powlys churche | yarde.

Collation. x⁴, A–X, AA–TT⁴ ; 164 leaves.

Leaf 1ᵃ Title, 1ᵇ Woodcuts, 2ᵃ Prologue, 2ᵇ–4ᵇ Table, 5ᵃ–163ᵇ Text, 164ᵃ Woodcut, 164ᵇ Woodcut. [*B.L.*]   [1246.]

This copy wants title-page and last four leaves, and leaves 2, 3, 4 have been misbound at end.

DONATUS (AELIUS).   Donatus pro pueris.
4to.   *Richard Pynson.* [*London.*] [1498.]

Title. Donatus pro pueris | [Woodcut]. Leaf 2ᵃ. pArtes orationis quot sunt ? octo. que ? | nomē, pronomē, verbum, aduerbium | participiū [*etc.*] Leaf 12ᵃ, line 26. in ordine . Cuius significationis dolentis . quia dolo= | rem mentis significat. | Finis.

Collation. a, b⁶ ; 12 leaves. 29 lines. No headlines or numbers to pages.

Leaf 1ᵃ Title, 1ᵇ blank, 2ᵃ–12ᵃ Text, 12ᵇ Device. [*B.L.*]   [1305¹.]

The woodcut on the title-page depicts a master with eight pupils.

No other copy is known.

DONATUS (AELIUS).   Accidence.
4°.   *Wynkyn de Worde.   Westminster* [1499.]

Leaf 1ᵃ.   ℂ Accedence | [1 line space] | HOw many partis of reason ben the | re (eyght) whiche. viii. Nowne, Pro- | nowne, Verbe, Aduerbe, Partycyple, | Cōiunccion, preposicion, Interieccyō | ℂ How many ben declynyd ; & how | many ben undeclynyd. [*etc.*]   Leaf 13ᵇ *Colophon.* ℂ Prynted at westmynstre In Caxtons | hous by wynkyn de worde. | Leaf 14ᵃ blank.   Leaf 14ᵇ Woodcut.

Collation. A⁸, B⁶ ; 14 leaves.   29 lines.   With headlines ; no numbers to pages.   [*B.L.*]
Woodcut on last page of master and three pupils.   **[1305².]**

ECKIUS (JOANNES) [Johann Maier].   Contra Lutherum.
4to.   *Marcel Franck.   Rome,* 1523.

Title. ASSERITVR HIC INVICTISSIMI ANGLIAE | regis liber de sacramentis, a calumniis & | impietatibus Ludderi, | Iohanne Eckio | Autore. | [Woodcut of arms of England.] | Ad fidei catholicæ defensionem & | inclytissimi Angliæ regis | honorem.   Leaf 47ᵇ *Colophon.*   Excusum in alma urbe Rhoma typis Marcelli | Franck Germani, Adriano. VI. Pontifice, & | Carolo. V. Imperatore, Reip. Christianæ | præsidentibus, Mense Maio | Anno Salut. | 1523.

Collation. A–M⁴ ; 48 leaves.   28 lines.   No headlines or numbers to pages.

Leaf 1ᵃ Title, 1ᵇ blank, 2ᵃ–3ᵃ Dedication to Wilhelmus Bp. of Enckenfurt, 3ᵇ Julius Simon in Lutherum, 4 blank, 5ᵃ–47ᵇ Text, 48ᵃ Errata, 48ᵇ blank.   [*R.L.*]   **[1481³.]**
One of the many controversial works following the publication of Henry's Assertio septem sacramentorum in 1521.

EDGEWORTH (ROGER).   Sermons. 4to. *Robert Caly.   London,* 1557.

Title [within borders].   Sermons | very fruitfull, godly, | and learned, preached and | sette foorth by Maister Roger | Edgeworth, doctoure of diuini- | tie, Canon of the Cathedrall | churches of Sarisburie, Welles | and Bristow, residentiary in the | Cathedrall churche of Welles, | and Chauncellour of the same | churche : With a repertorie | or table, directinge to ma- | ny notable matters ex- | pressed in the same | sermons. | ℂ Excusum Londini in ædibus Roberti | Caly, Tipographi, Mense Septemb. | Anno. 1557.   Leaf 331ᵇ *Colophon.*   ℂ Imprinted at | London by Robert Calye, within | the precinct of Christes | Hospitall. | Cum priuilegio ad impri- mendum | solum.

Collation.   +⁴, A⁴, B⁶, A–Z, Aa–Zz, Aaa–Zzz, Aaaa–Iiii⁴, Kkkk⁶; 332 leaves.   32 lines.   With headlines and numbers to pages.

Leaf 1ᵃ Title, 1ᵇ Verse, 2ᵃ–3ᵇ Preface, 4ᵃ Contents, 4ᵇ blank, 5ᵃ–14ᵇ Table, 15ᵃ–331ᵃ Text, 331ᵇ Colophon, 332 blank.   [*B.L.*]   [**1285.**]

ELYOT (SIR THOMAS).   Dictionary.   fol.   *T. Berthelet. London,* 1542.
Last leaf only, containing the last page of the Dictionary and the colophon.   [Device.] 🙠 Londini 🙡 | In officina Thomae Ber- | theleti typis impres. | cum privilegio ad impri- | mendum solum. | Anno M.D.XLII | 🙢 | [**1978².**]
No complete copy of this edition is known.   Besides this last leaf, of which only this copy is known, the Bodleian possesses five leaves contain- ing the title, proheme to Henry VIII, an address to the reader and a table of errata, all printed on vellum.

Herbert, 441.   W. W. Greg, Thomas Berthelet (Bibl. Soc., Handlists of English Printers, III), p. 9.

ELYOT (SIR THOMAS).   Pasquil the plain.
                    8º.   *Thomas Berthelet. London,* 1532.
Title. PASQVIL | THE | PLAYNE. | LONDINI IN ÆDIBVS | THOMAE BERTHELETI. | M.D.XXXII.   Ends leaf 30ᵇ.   Adieu | gentil herers, and saye well by Pas- | quill, whan he is from you. | CVM PRIVILEGIO.
Collation.   A–C⁸, D⁶; 30 leaves.   24 lines.   With headlines and numbers to pages.

Leaf 1ᵃ Title, 1ᵇ–2ᵇ To the readers, 3ᵃ–30ᵇ text.   [*B.L.*]   [**368⁴.**]

ERASMUS (DESIDERIUS).   Book of good manners.
                    8º.   *John Waley. London,* 1554.
[*Title.* DE CIVILI- | TATE MORVM PVERILIVM | per des. Erasmum Roterodamum, Libellus nunc | primum conditus & æditus. | Roberto VVhitintoni | interprete. | A lytle booke of good maners for chyl- | dren, now lately compiled and put forth | by Erasmus Roterodam in latin | tongue with interpretation of | the same into the vulgare | englyshe tongue, by | Robert VVhit- | tinton Poet | Laureat. | (∴)]

Leaf 28ᵃ *Colophon.*   Thus endeth this litle booke of good ma- | ners. Imprinted at London in Foster | Lane by John UUallye | Anno M.D.Ljjjj.

Collation. A–C⁸, D⁴ ; 28 leaves. 26 and 36 lines. No headlines or numbers to pages.

Leaf 1ᵃ Title, 1ᵇ blank, 2ᵃ–28ᵃ Text, 28ᵇ blank.   **[209⁴.]**

Wants the first leaf.

ERASMUS (DESIDERIUS). [De morte declamatio.]
8°.   *Thomas Berthelet.   London* [1532.]

Title [within border].   A treatise perswadynge | a man patientlye to | suffre the deth of | his frende.   Leaf 20ᵇ *Colophon.*   Thomas Berthelet regius impressor | excudebat.   Cum priuilegio.

Collation. A, B⁸, C⁴ ; 20 leaves. 23 lines. No headlines or numbers to pages.

Leaf 1ᵃ Title, 1ᵇ Verses, 2ᵃ–20ᵇ Text.   [*B.L.*]   **[368³.]**

——— De octo orationis partium constructione libellus.
8°.   *Freiburg,* 1534.

Title. ✢ DE OCTO | ORATIONIS PARTIVM CON- | structione libellus perelegans, authore Desi | derio ERASMO ROTERO. | Scholiis Henrici Primæi apud Mo | nasterienses gymnasiarchæ | illustratus | ⚥ | [Device of J. Faber].   Leaf 47ᵇ *Colophon.*   FRIBVRGI BRISGOIAE | M. D. XXXIIII. | EXCVDEBAT IOANNES FABER | EMMEVS IVLIACENSIS.

Collation. A–F⁸ ; 48 leaves. 26 lines. With headlines ; no numbers to pages.

Leaf 1ᵃ Title, 1ᵇ H. Primaeus to the reader, 2ᵃ Colet to Lily, 2ᵇ–3ᵃ Erasmus to the readers, 3ᵇ–47ᵃ Text, 47ᵇ Colophon. [*Rom. & Ital. L.*]

Wants last leaf.   **[424².]**

ERRA PATER. Prognostication.   8°.   *Robert Wyer.   London.*

Title.   Pronostication | For euer, of Erra Pater, | a Iewe borne in Iewery, a | Doctoure in Astronomye, | and Physycke Profy- | table to kepe the body | in helth, And also | Pholomeus sayth | the same. | Erra Pater. | This Pronostycacion ser- | [woodcut] | ueth for all the worlde ouer.   Leaf 16ᵇ *Colophon.*   ⊄ Imprynted by | me Robert Wyer, dwellynge | at the sygne of S. Johñ | Euangelyst, in | Seyncte | Martyns parysshe. | in the Duke of Suf- | folkes rentes, be | syde charynge Crosse. | Cum priuilegio, ad | imprimendum | Solum. | [Name label].

Collation. AB⁸; 16 leaves. 22–3 lines. With headlines; no numbers to pages.

Leaf 1ᵃ Title, 1ᵇ–16ᵃ Text, 16ᵇ Colophon. [*B.L.*]   [209⁶.]

Two other editions by Wyer are described by Plomer [Nos. 25, 86] but this does not agree with either.

ESTIENNE (CHARLES). De re hortensi libellus.
                     8°. *M. and G. Trechsel. Lyons,* 1536.
Title. DE RE HOR | TENSI LIBELLVS VVL | GARIA HERBARVM, FLORVM, AC | fruticum, qui in hortis conseri so- | lent, nomina Latinis uocibus | efferre docens ex proba- | tis autoribus. | In puerorum gratiam atꝗ utilitatem. | [Device] | LVGDVNI, | APVD HÆREDES SIMONIS | VINCENTII | M.D.XXXVI. | Leaf 51ᵇ *Colophon.* EXCVDEBANT LVGDV | NI MELCHIOR ET | GASPAR TRECHSEL | FRATRES. 1536.

Collation. a–f⁸, g⁴; 52 leaves. 31 lines. With headlines and numbers to pages.

Leaf 1ᵃ Title, 1ᵇ blank, 2 Preface of C. Stephanus, 3ᵃ–41ᵇ Text, 42ᵃ–44ᵇ Annotationes, 45ᵃ–51ᵇ Indices, 52 blank. [*R.L.*]   [419³.]

FIORI (GIACOMO). Adversus M. Lutheri dogmata.
                     4to. *Antonius Bladus. Rome,* 1525.
Title. AD CLEMENTEM SEPTI- | MVM PONTIFICEM | MAXIMVM | IACOBI FLORI PRAESBY- | teri samnitis aduersus Impia & | pestifera Martini lutheri | dogmata præfatio. Leaf 16ᵇ *Colophon.* ℂ Impressum Rome apud Antonium Bladū de | Asula die. viii. Mensis Iulii. M.D.XXV.

Collation. a–d⁴; 16 leaves. 27 lines. No headlines or numbers to pages.

Leaf 1ᵃ Title, 1ᵇ blank, 2 Letter to Matthaeus Tigurtinus, 3ᵃ–16ᵇ Text. [*R.L.*]   [1481⁴.]

FISHER (JOHN). Fruitful sayings of David.
                     4to. *Wynkyn de Worde. London,* 1509.
Title [Woodcut]. ℂ This treatyse concernynge the fruytful | saynges of Dauyd the kynge & prophete in | the seuen penytencyall psalmes. Deuyded | in seuen sermons was made and compyled | by the ryght reuerente fader in god Johan | fyssher doctoure of dyuynyte and bysshop

of | Rochester at the exortacion and sterynge of | the moost excellēt princesse Margarete coū | tesse of Rychemoūt and Derby, & moder to | our souerayne lorde kynge Henry the . vij.   Leaf 146ᵃ *Colophon*.   ℂ Here endeth the exposycyon of the .vii. psalmes.   En- | prynted at London in the Fletestrete at the sygne of the | sonne, by Wynkyn de Worde prynter vnto the moost ex- | cellent pryncesse my lady the kynges graūdame.   In the | yere of our lorde god . M.CCCCC . and . ix . the . xij . daye | of the moneth of Juyn.

Collation. aa⁸, bb⁴, cc–yy⁸/⁴, zz⁸, &·&·⁶ ; 146 leaves.   32 lines.   No headlines or numbers to pages.

Leaf 1ᵃ Title, 1ᵇ Prologue, 2ᵃ–146ᵃ Text, 146ᵇ W. de Worde's device. [*B.L.*]   [1036¹.]

FLOWER OF THE COMMANDMENTS OF GOD.
fol.   *Wynkyn de Worde.   London*, 1510.

Leaf 1ᵃ.   Ihesus | ℂ The floure of the commaundementes of god with many exam- | ples and auctorytees extracte and drawen as well of holy scryptures | as of other doctours and good auncient faders, the whiche is moche | vtyle and prouffytable vnto all people. | [*etc.*].   Leaf 288ᵃ *Colophon*.   Emprynted at London in Flete strete | at the sygne of the sonne by Wynkyn | de Worde.   The secōde yere of yᵉ reygne | of oure moost naturell souerayne lorde | kynge Henry the eyght of that name. | Fynysshed the yere of oure lorde. M. | CCCCC. x. the xiiii. daye of Septem | bre :

Collation. A–D, A–Z, Aa–Xx⁶ ; 288 leaves.   43 lines.   With headlines and numbers to pages.

Leaf 1ᵃ Title, 1ᵇ Cut of Crucifixion, 2ᵃ Prologue of the translator, 2ᵇ–24ᵃ Table, 24ᵇ blank, 25ᵃ–288ᵃ Text, 288ᵇ W. de Worde's device 5.   [*B.L.*]
[2001.]

Translated by Andrew Chertsey from La fleur des commandemens de Dieu, first published at Rouen in 1496 and frequently reprinted.

FOUNDATION OF THE CHAPEL OF WALSINGHAM.
4to.   *Richard Pynson.*   [*London.*]   [1496.]

Leaf 2ᵃ.   ℂ Of this chapell se here the fundacyon | Bylded the yere of crystes incarnacyon | A thousande complete syxty and one | The tyme of sent edward kyng of this region | [*etc.*]   Leaf 4ᵇ line 1.   O gracyous lady glory of Jerusalem | Cypresse of syon and ioye of Israel | Rose of Jeryco and sterre of Bethleem | O gloryous lady our askynge nat repell | In mercy all wymèn euer thou doste excell | Therfore blissid lady graunt thou thy great grace | To all that the deuoutly visyte in this place. | ⊄ Amen | [Pynson's device 3].

Collation. [a⁴]; 4 leaves, 31 lines. No headlines or numbers to pages.

Leaf 1 not known, 2ᵃ–4ᵇ Text, 4ᵇ device. [*B.L.*]   [1254⁶.]

No other copy known. The first leaf probably contained a short title and a woodcut. From R. Smith's sale, 1682.

FROISSART (JEAN).   Chronicles of England.   Vol. I.
    fol.   *William Middleton.*   *London* [1545.]
    Title [within borders].   HEre begynneth the fyrst | volum of Syr Iohan Froyssart : of the Cro- | nycles of Englande, Fraunce, Spayne, Por | tyngale, Scotlaunde, Bretayne, Flaunders : | and other places adioynynge.   Trans- lated | out of frenche into our materall [*sic*] Englysshe | tonge, by Iohan Bouchier knyght lorde Berners : At the cōmaundement of our moste highe redou- | ted souerayne lorde kynge Henry the . VIII . kynge of En | glande, Fraũce, & Irelande defēdour of the fayth | and of the churche of Englande and | also of Irelande in earth the | supreme heade. | [Type ornaments.] Leaf 332ᵃ *Colophon.*   Thus endeth the firste volume of sir | Iohan Froissart : of the cronicles of England. | . . . . . . Imprinted at | London in Fletestrete at the sygne of the Geor- | ge by Wyllyam Myddylton.

Collation.   A⁶, B⁴, a–v, aa–vv, aaa–nnn⁶, ooo⁴; 332 leaves.   54 lines. With headlines and numbers to pages.

Leaf 1ᵃ Title, 1ᵇ Woodcut of royal arms, 2 Preface, 3ᵃ–10ᵃ Index, 10ᵇ blank, 11ᵃ–332ᵃ Text, 332ᵇ blank.   [2412.]

Signatures dd and ee are misplaced.

—— Chronicles of England.   Vol. II.
    fol.   *Richard Pynson. London,* 1525.
    Title [within border].   ⊄ Here begynneth the thirde | and fourthe boke of sir Iohñ Frois- | sart of the cronycles of Englande, | Fraunce, Spaygne, Portyngale, | Scotlande, Bretayne, Flaunders, | and other places adioynyng, trans- | lated out of Frenche in to englysshe | by Iohan Bouchier knyght lorde | Berners, deputie generall of yᵉ kyn | ges towne of Calais and marchesse | of the same, at the cōmaundement of | our most highe redouted souerayne | lorde kyng Henry the eight, kynge | of Englande and of Fraũce & highe | defender of the Christen faith. &c.   Leaf 334ᵃ *Colophon.* ⊄ Thus endeth the thirde and fourthe boke of sir Iohñ Fro- | issart, of the

cronycles of Englande [*etc.*]. . . . . . Imprinted at London in Fletestrete by Richarde Pynson, | printer to the kynges moost noble grace.   And ended the last | day of August : the yere of our lorde god. M.D.xxv. | ℭ Cum priuylegio a rege indulto.

Collation.   a⁸, A–V, AA–VV, AAA–NNN⁶, OOO⁸; 334 leaves.   52 lines. With headlines and numbers to pages.

Leaf 1ᵃ Title, 1ᵇ Woodcut of Royal arms, 2ᵃ Preface, 2ᵇ–8ᵃ Table, 8ᵇ blank, 9ᵃ–334ᵃ Text, 334ᵇ Pynson's armorial device.   **[2412.]**

With early antograph inscription "Smyth p̄cii xxx⁹."

The bibliography of the editions by Pynson and Middleton is very confusing and has never been properly worked out.   Middleton reprinted the second volume exactly, down to the colophon, so that it is usually confused with Pynson's edition.   In both editions there appear to be variations of the title-page.

G. (J.).   The mirror or looking glass of life.
                                8⁰. [*Robert Wyer.*] [*London*, 1550.]

Title.   ℭ Here begyn- | neth a lytell treatyse called, or | named the (Myrrour or lokynge | glasse of lyfe) Expedyent and | necessarye, for any Crysten | man to beholde or loke in, | for cŏfortyng of the soule | whiche desyreth the | lyfe eternall. | ℭ Verbum domini : manet in eternum. | The worde of god, shall euer endure. | [Woodcut.]   End not known.

Collation.   a⁸, b–m⁴; 52 leaves.

Leaf 1ᵃ Title, 1ᵇ–5ᵃ John G unto the reader, 5ᵇ–7ᵇ Index of chapters, 8ᵃ–   Text.   **[19¹.]**

A small woodcut of the Crucifixion on the title-page.

Imperfect, wanting all after leaf 52.

The two other copies known to me, in the Cambridge University Library and the Bodleian, both also end with page 52.

Not mentioned by Plomer.

GEOFFREY OF MONMOUTH.   Britanniae regum et principum origo.
                        4to. *J. Badius Ascensius.   Paris*, 1508.

Title.   Britānie vtiiusqₑ | regū & prīcipū Ori | go & gesta insignia | ab Galfrido Monumetensi ex antiquissi- | mis Britannici sermonis monumentis in | latinū sermonē traducta : & ab Ascensio cu | ra & impēdio magistri Iuonis Cauellati in | lucem edita : p̄stant in eiusdem ædibus. | [Device of Badius.]   Ends leaf 199^b.   Ex ædibus nostris Ad idus Iulias Anni MDVIII.

Collation.   AA, A–M^8, N^6;   110 leaves.   33 lines.   With headlines and numbers to pages.

Leaf 1^a Title, 1^b–2^a Letter of Ivo Cavellat, 2^b verses, 3^a–6^b Table, 7^a Alani carmen, 7^b Alanus to Ivo Cavellat, 8^a Galfridus to the Duke of Chester, 8^b Cavellat to the Reader, 9^a–109^b Text. [*R.L.*]   **[1511.]**

Wants last leaf, blank ?

GRAMMAR.   8°.   [*Antwerp.*]   [1535.]

Begins : DE NOMI- | NIBVS HETEROCLI- | TIS. | ☞ Defectiua in casu & numero. | [*etc.*]   A 5 begins : REGVLAE VERSI- | FICALES. | [*etc.*]

A^8?   27 lines.   No headlines or numbers to pages.   [*R.T.*]   **[424^6.]**

Fragment of some grammar, perhaps Lily's.

Wants all after A^6.

HALLE (EDWARD).   [Union of the two families of York and Lancaster.]   fol.   *R. Grafton. London,* 1550.

Fol. 1 of this copy begins : ℂ An introduction into the History of | Kyng Henry the fourthe.   *Colophon.*   ℂ Imprynted at London by | Rychard Grafton, Prynter to the Kynges Maiestye. | 1550. | Cum privilegio imprimendum solum.

Collation.   A^4, A^8, B–E^6, ff^2, a–g^6, h^8, I^2, a–q^6, r^8, s^4, A–I^6, K^8, L (three leaves), AA–DD^6, aa–ee^6, ff^8, aaa–iii^6, kkk^8, lll^4, a–z^6, A–Z^6.

Leaf 1^a Title, 2–4 introductory matter.   Fol. i–xxxii+[2] (Henry IV), i–L + [2] (Henry V), i–Cii + [4] (Henry VI), i–lxi + [4] (Edward IV), i–xxiiii (Edward V), i–xxxv + [1] (Richard III), i–lxi + [5] (Henry VII), i–ccLxiii + [13] (Henry VIII).   **[1978^1]**

This copy wants the first four leaves, A^2 of Henry IV, possibly L^4 of of Edward IV (probably blank), and the last seven leaves (containing table and colophon).   It has been made up with manuscript.

For the last leaf of Elyot's Dictionary, 1542, bound at end of this volume, *see* ELYOT.

Herbert 530–1.   There is a full bibliographical description of the three issues of this book in Lowndes *Bibl. Man.* ii. 983.

HARDING (JOHN).   Chronicle.   4to.   *Richard Grafton.   London,* 1543.

Title [within borders].   ❧ The chroni- | cle of Jhon Hardyng, from | the firste begynnyng of Englande, vnto the | reigne of kyng Edward the fourth wher he | made an end of his chronicle.   And from that | tyme is added a continuacion of the | storie in prose to this our tyme, | now first imprinted, gathe- | red out of diuerse and | sondery autours | y^t haue writē | of the af- | faires | of Englande. | LONDINI | Ex officina Richardi Graftoni. | Mense Ianuarii. | MD.xliii. | Cum priuilegio ad impri- | mendum solum. | Leaf 386^b *Colophon.* [Printer's device] LONDINI. | Ex officina Richardi Graftoni, | Cum priuilegio ad im- | primendum solum | per septennium.

Collation.   [8] a–z, A–F⁸, G⁶, Aa–Ss⁸, Tt² ; 386 leaves.   33 lines.   With headlines and numbers to pages.

Leaf 1ª Title, 1ᵇ blank, 2ª–4ᵇ Grafton's dedication to Thomas, Duke of Norfolk, 5ª–8ᵇ Preface, 9ª–13ª Proheme of Harding, 13ᵇ–240ᵇ Harding's Chronicle, 241ª Title, 241ᵇ To the reader, 242ª–386ª Continuation of Chronicle, 386ᵇ Colophon.   [*B.L.*]   [**1442.**]

Delivered to Pepys, June 30, 1688, by Robert Scott the bookseller, price 6.s.   See Scott's letter, correspondence in Colburn's 1828 edition of Diary, pp. 137-8.

HAWES (STEPHEN).   The example of virtue.
                                         4to.   *Wynkyn de Worde.*   [*London,* 1510.]
Title.   ꝗ Here begynneth the boke called the ex- | ample of vertu. | [Woodcut.]   Ends 46ᵇ: For to dystyll the dewe of influence | Upon my brayn so dull and rude | And to enlumyn me with his sapyence | That I my rudnes may exclude | And in my mater well to conclude | Unto thy pleasure and to the reders all | To whome I excuse me now in generall | Explicit exemplum virtutis | [W. de Worde's device 9.]

Collation.   aa–ff⁸ʲ⁴, gg⁶, hh⁴, ; 46 leaves.   No headlines or numbers to pages.
Leaf 1ª Title, 1ᵇ blank, 2 Table, 3 Prologue, 4ª–46ᵇ Text.   [*B.L.*]
                                                                          [**1254².**]
Numerous woodcuts.   The only copy known.

HEAVENLY ACT.   8º.   *Robert Wyer.   London.*   [1550.]
Title.   ꝗ An Heauenly | Acte concernyn- | ge howe man | shall lyue, made by oure | Soueraygne Lorde | GOD the Father, | God the Sone, | and God the holy Ghost, | And all the whole | clergye in heauen |

consentynge to | the same | Parlyament, as | it sheweth | hereafter. Leaf 14ᵇ *Colophon.* ❡ Imprynted by me | Robert wyer. | ❡ Cum priuilegio regali, | Ad imprimendum solum. | [Wyer's device.]

Collation. AB⁴, C⁶ ; 14 leaves. 24 lines. No headlines or pagination.

Leaf 1ᵃ Title, 1ᵇ Names of the Lordes, 2ᵃ–14ᵃ Text, 14ᵇ colophon and device. [*B.L.*]   [**75²**.]

Not mentioned by Plomer.

HENRY VIII.   Assertio septem sacramentorum.
                         4to.   *Stephanus Guilliretus.   Rome,* 1521.
Title [within border].   LIBRVM HVNC INVICTISS. | ANGLIÆ REGIS FIDEI DE- | FENSORIS CONTRA | MART. LVTHERVM | LEGENTIBVS, DE- | CEM ANNORVM | ET TOTIDEM | XL. INDVL- | GENTIA APOSTOLICA | AVTHORITATE | CONCESSA | EST. | Cum Gratia | et privilegio.   Leaf 5ᵃ [within border].   ASSERTIO SE- | ptē Sacramētoᴤ ad- | uersus Marti . Lu- | the℞, aedita ab in- | uictissimo An- | gliæ & Franciæ | rege, & do. | Hyberniæ Henrico | eius nominis | octauo.   Leaf 89ᵇ *Colophon.* ❡ Romæ, opera Stephani Guillireti, | mense Decembri. M.D. | XXI. apostolica | Sede vacan- | te.

Collation.   [4] a–v⁴, x⁶, y⁴, z² ; 96 leaves. 25 lines. No headlines or numbers to pages.

Leaf 1ᵃ Title, 1ᵇ Verses, 2ᵃ–4ᵃ Letter of Pope Leo X to Henry, 4ᵇ blank, 5ᵃ Title, 5ᵇ blank, 6ᵃ–8ᵇ Henry's addresses to Leo X and the readers, 9ᵃ–89ᵇ Text, 90 blank, 91ᵃ–96ᵃ Oration of Clerk, 96ᵇ Answer of Leo X. [*R.L.*]   [**1481¹**.]

The original edition of the Assertio was issued by Pynson on July 12, 1521. Copies on vellum were sent to Leo X, who on Oct. 11th issued a bull conferring on Henry the title of Fidei defensor. The book was immediately reprinted at Rome by command of the Pope, and besides the text contained Clerk's oration, Henry's addresses to Leo X and the readers, the papal bull, etc., and is thus the first complete edition of the book. The prefatory matter was printed separately by Pynson and is found added to some copies of the Assertio of 1521.

——   A necessary doctrine.   4to.   *Thomas Berthelet.   London,* 1543.
Title [within borders].   A NECES- | SARY DOCTRINE | AND ERVDITION FOR | ANY CHRISTEN | man, sette furthe by | the kynges ma- | iestie of En- | glande | &c. | ❖ | Psal. xix. | Lorde preserue the Kyng, and here | vs whan we call vpon the. | Psal. xx. | Lorde in thy

strengthe the Kynge | shall rejoise, and be meruailous glad | through thy saluation. | T.B.   Leaf 98^b *Colophon*.   ⚓ IMPRINTED at London in Fletestrete | by Thomas Barthelet printer to the | kynges hyghnes, the . XXIX. | day of May, the yere of our | Lorde. M.D.XLIII. | CVM priuilegio ad imprimendum solum.

Collation. A⁴, A–Y⁴, Z⁶ ; 98 leaves. 34 lines. With headlines and numbers to pages.

Leaf 1^a Title, 1^b Contents, 2^a–4^a Preface, 4^b blank, 5^a–98^b Text.   [*B.L.*]
                                                                            [**1757.**]

A printed notice in the book states "This boke bounde in paper bourdes or in claspes, not to be solde aboue . XVI. d."

HEROLD (JOANNES).   De bello sacro continuatae historiae libri VI.
                    fol.   *N. Brylinger and J. Oporinus.   Basle* [1549.]
Title.   DE BELLO SACRO | CONTINVATAE HISTORIAE, LIBRI VI. COM- | mentariis rerum Syriacarum Guilhelmi Tyrensis Archiepiscopi, | additi. [*etc.*] . . . | IOANNE HEROLD HOECHSTET- | tensi authore. | . . . | BASILEAE.

Collation. a⁴, a–v⁶, x⁸ ; 132 leaves. 45 lines. With headlines and numbers to pages.

Leaf 1^a Title, 1^b List of authorities, 2^a–4^b Preface, 5^a–131^a Text, 131^b, 132 blank. [*R.L.*]   [**2270².**]

Bound up with the Historia belli sacri of William of Tyre, to which it forms a continuation.

With the autograph of Robert Burton.

HEYWOOD (JOHN).   The pardoner and the frere.
                  fol.   *William Rastell.   [London.]* 1533.
Leaf 1^a begins : ⸿ A mery play betwene | the pardoner and the freere, the curate | and neybour Pratte. | [*etc.*]   Leaf 8^b *Colophon*.   Imprynted by Wyllyam Rastell the .v. day | of Apryll, the yere of our Lorde .M. | CCCCC.xxxIII. | ⸿ Cum priuilegio.

Collation. AB⁴ ; 8 leaves. 42 lines. No headlines or numbers to pages.

Leaf 1^a–8^b Text. [*B.L.*]   [**1977⁴.**]

HEYWOOD (JOHN).   John the husbande, Tyb his wife.

fol.   *William Rastell.*   [*London.*] 1533.

Leaf 1 begins : [Border piece] ℂ A mery play | betwene Johan Johan the | husbande, Tyb his | wyfe, & syr Jhān | the preest. | [Border piece.] | [*etc.*].   Leaf 8ᵇ *Colophon.*   ℂ Impryntyd by Wyllyam Rastell, the . xii . day of | February the yere of our lord.   M. ccccc . and xxxiii. | ℂ Cum priuilegio.

Collation.   AB⁴ ; 8 leaves.   44 lines.   No headlines or numbers to pages.

Leaf 1ᵃ–8ᵇ Text.   [*B.L.*]   [**1977** ³.]

------ The play of the wether.   fol.   *William Rastell.*   [*London.*] 1533.

Title.   ℂ The play of the wether | [Border piece] | ℂ A new and a very | mery enterlude of | all maner we | thers made | by Johñ Heywood, | [Border piece]. | The players names. | Jupiter a god. | Mery reporte the vyce. | The gentylman. | The marchaunt. | The ranger. | The water myller. | The wynde miller. | The gentylwoman. | The launder. | A boy the lest that can play. | ⬬ ⬬ ⬬ | Leaf 18ᵃ *Colophon.*   Prynted by w. Rastell. | 1533. | Cum priuilegio.

Collation.   A—C⁴, D⁶ ; 18 leaves.   40 lines.   No headlines or numbers to pages.

Leaf 1ᵃ Title, 1ᵇ blank, 2ᵃ–18ᵃ Text, 18ᵇ blank.   [*B.L.*]   [**1977²**.]

------ A play of love.   fol.   *William Rastell.*   [*London.*] 1534.

Title [within border].   A play of loue, | ℂ A newe and a | mery enterlude concernyng plea- | sure and payne in loue, | made by Jhoñ | Heywood. | .∵. | The players | names. | .∵. | A man a louer not beloued.   A woman beloued not louyng, | A man a louer and beloued. | The vyse nother louer nor beloued.   Leaf 20ᵃ *Colophon.*   Prynted by . w. Rastell | M . ccccc . xxxiiii. | Cum priuilegio Regali.

Collation.   A–E⁴ ; 20 leaves.   46 lines.   No headlines or numbers to pages.

Leaf 1ᵃ Title, 1ᵇ blank, 2ᵃ–20ᵃ Text, 20ᵇ blank.   [*B.L.*]   [**1977¹**.]

------ Of gentleness and nobility.   fol.   *John Rastell.*   [*London.*] [1532.]

Leaf 1ᵃ begins : ℂ Of Gentylnes & Nobylyte | A dyaloge betwen the marchaũt the | Knyght & the plowman dysputyng who is a verey | gentylman & who is a noble man and how men | shuld come to auctoryte, compilid in maner of an | enterlude with diuers toys & gestis addyd therto |

to make mery pastyme and disport. | [*etc.*]. Leaf 14ᵇ *Colophon.* Johēs rastell me fieri fecit | Cum priuilegio regali. | [Two border pieces].

Collation. A⁶, BC⁴ ; 14 leaves. 44 lines. No headlines or numbers to pages.

Leaf 1ᵃ–14ᵇ Text. [*B.L.*] **[1977 ⁵.]**

HEYWOOD (JOHN). An hundred epigrams.
8°. *Thomas Powell. London*, 1556.

Title [within border]. ⚘ An hundred | Epi- | grammes. | Inuented and | made | by | Iohn Hey- | wood. | Anno Christi. | M.D.L.VI. Leaf 24ᵃ *Colophon.* IMPRINTED at London in Flete- | strete, by Thomas Powell. | Cum priuilegio ad imprimen- | dum solum.

Collation. A–C⁸ ; 24 leaves. 30 lines. With headlines, no numbers to pages.

Leaf 1ᵃ Title, 1ᵇ To the Reader, 2ᵃ–3ᵇ Table, 4ᵃ–23ᵇ Epigrams, 24ᵃ colophon, 24ᵇ blank. [*B.L.*] **[412 ¹.]**

—— The spider and the fly. 4to. *Thomas Powell. London*, 1556.

Title [within border]. THE SPIDER | and the Flie. | ⚹ | A parable of the Spider | and the Flie, made by | John Heywood. | ⚹ | IMPRINTED AT | LONDON IN FLETE | STRETE BY THO. | POWELL. | ❦ | ANNO. 1556. | T.P. Leaf 228ᵇ *Colophon.* ❧ IMPRINTED AT LON-❧ | DON IN FLETE- | STRETE, BY THO. | POVVELL. | ⚹ | Cum priuilegio ad imprimen- | dum solum.

Collation. A–C⁴, A–Z⁴, Aa⁴ ⁽⁺¹²⁾¹⁶, Bb⁴ ⁽⁺²⁾⁶, Cc⁴ ⁽⁺⁴⁾⁸, Dd⁴ ⁽⁺⁸⁾¹², Ee⁴ ⁽⁺¹²⁾¹⁶, Ff⁴ ⁽⁺¹⁰⁾¹⁴, Gg⁴ ⁽⁺⁴⁾⁸, Hh–SS⁴ ; 228 leaves. With headlines, no numbers to pages.

Leaf 1ᵃ Title, 1ᵇ Portrait of Heywood, 2ᵃ–3ᵇ Preface, 4ᵃ–11ᵇ Table, 12ᵃ Portrait of Heywood, 12ᵇ Introduction, 13ᵃ–225ᵃ Text, 225ᵇ–228ᵃ Conclusion, 228ᵇ colophon. [*B.L.*] **[1099.]**

The curious collation of this book results from the interpolation of a large number of woodcuts occupying two pages and depicting the battles of the flies and the spiders, who represented the Catholics and Protestants.

HIGDEN (RANULPH). Polycronicon.
fol. *William Caxton. Westminster*, 1482.

Leaf 2ᵃ Prohemye. gRete thankynges lawde & honoure we merytoryous- | ly ben bounde to yelde and offre vnto wryters of hys- | toryes, whiche gretely haue prouffyted oure mortal | lyf.   Leaf 449ᵃ, line 21.   Ended the second day of Iuyll the xxij yere of | the regne of kynge Edward the fourth & of the Incarnacion of | our lord a thousand four honderd foure score and tweyne, | Fynysshed per Caxton.

Collation. ab⁸, c⁴, 1–28⁸, 28*², 29–48⁸, 49⁴, 50, 52–55⁸ ; 450 leaves. 40 lines.   With headlines and numbers to pages [often incorrect].

Leaf 1 blank, 2ᵃ–3ᵇ Prologue, 4ᵃ–20ᵃ Index, 20ᵇ, 21 blank, 22ᵃ–24ᵃ Dialogue between John of Trevisa and Lord Berkeley, 24ᵃ–24ᵇ Letter from John of Trevisa to Lord Berkeley, 25 blank, 26ᵃ–449ᵃ Text, 449ᵇ, 450 blank. [*B.L.*]   [2063.]

This copy wants seven leaves.

HOOPER (JOHN).   An oversight upon Jonas.
8°. *John Day and William Seres.   London* [1550.]

Title [within border].   An ouersight | and deliberacion v | pon the holy Prophete | Jonas : made, and vtte | red before the kynges | maiestie, and his moost | honorable councell, by Ihon Hoper in lent | last past. Compre- | hended in seuē | Sermons. | Anno.M | D.L. | Excepte ye repente, ye | shall al peryshe. | Luke . xiii. | Cum priuilegio ad impri |

mendum solum. Leaf 192ᵇ *Colophon.*   ¶ Imprinted | at London by

Ihon | Daye, dwellyng ouer Al- | dersgate, and Wyl- | liam Seres dwel | linge in Peter | Colledge. | Cum priuilegio ad impri | mendum solum.

Collation.   +, A–Z⁸ ; 192 leaves.   22 lines.   With headlines and numbers to pages.

Leaf 1ᵃ Title, 1ᵇ blank, 2ᵃ–9ᵇ Epistle to Edward VI, 10ᵃ–191ᵇ Text, 192ᵃ Faults escaped, 192ᵇ *colophon.* [*B.L.*]   [55.]

This copy wants the last leaf.

INFORMATIO PUERORUM. 4to. *Richard Pynson.* [*London.*] [1499.]

Title. ¶ Libellulus, que Informatio pueroч appellatur | cum modico apparatu nouiter ɔpilatus . Incipit. | [Woodcut].   Leaf 19ᵇ line 19 . or after, or in the myddis | Finis | ¶ Emprynted by Richard Pynson.

Collation.   A⁶, B⁴, C⁶, D⁴ ; 20 leaves.   28 lines.   Without headlines or numbers to pages.

Leaf 1ᵃ Title, 1ᵇ blank, 2ᵃ–19ᵃ Text, 20 blank.   [*B.L.*]   [1305 ³.]

Woodcut of master and eight pupils.   The only copy known.

E

INTRODUCTORIUM LINGUAE LATINAE.
4to. [*Wynkyn de Worde*]. [*Westminster.*] 1495.

Title. ❡ Introductorium lingue latine. | [Woodcut]. Leaf 1ᵇ. ❡ Nominatiuo singularis. Primus . prima . primū. | genitiuo primi . prime . primi . &ᵒc̄ . sicut bonus . Sic re- | liqua sequentia declinantur. | ❡ Primus the fyrst . i . secūdus the seconde . ii . tercius | [*etc.*]. Leaf 36ᵇ, line 13. ❡ Hec media syllaba . quā nos solam posuimus a- | pud viros litteratores perraro reperī̃t breuis. | [De Worde's device].

Collation. A⁸, B–E⁶, F⁴ ; 36 leaves. 29 lines. With headlines and numbers to pages.

Leaf 1ª Title, 1ᵇ–2ª Declension of numerals, 2ᵇ Verses addressed to W.H. by Caius and Bernardus Andrae, 3ª–36ᵇ Text. [1305 ⁵.]

The woodcut on the title-page is of a master with three pupils. The author of this book, whose initials W.H. are given in the prefatory verses, was no doubt William Horman, the headmaster of Eton.

The date is found on leaf 1 verso. The only copy known.

JUSTES OF MAY AND JUNE, 1507. 4to. [*London.*] [1507.]

Title. ❡ Here begynneth the Iustes of the moneth | of Maye parfurnysshed & done by Char- | les brandon . Thomas knyuet . Gyles Ca | pell, & wyllyam Hussy. The . xxii . yere of | the reygne of our souerayne lorde kynge | Henry the seuenth. | [Type ornament] | Woodcut]. Leaf 5ª. ❡ Here begynneth the Iustes and tourney of yᵉ moneth | of June parfurnysshed and done by Rycharde Graye | erle of Kent, by Charles brandon wᵗ theyr two aydes | agaynst all comers . The . xxii . yere of the reygne of our | souerayne lorde kynge Henry yᵉ seuenth. | [Woodcut]. Ends leaf 10ª. The entrepryse was fondly vndertake | But it was done but onely for the sake | Of kynge Henry our naturall souerayne lorde | And of the prynce, who lyste it to remorde.

Collation. A⁶, B⁴ ; 10 leaves. No headlines or numbers to pages.

Leaf 1ª Title, 1ᵇ–4ᵇ Justs of May, 5ª–10ª Justs of June, 10ᵇ blank. [*B.L.*]. [1254 ¹.]

These two accounts, which form one book, not two as usually described, were probably printed soon after the events described took place. They are written in a very curious verse each stanza consisting of three long lines and one short, the three long lines all rhyming with the short line which ends the previous stanza.

KALENDAR.   [1.]
A small French block-printed kalendar on eleven leaves of vellum, designed for sailors, with maps of Brittany, Flanders, England and Ireland. Probably made in Brittany.

Autograph " F. Drak " on first leaf.

An English block-printed kalendar on a long narrow strip of vellum with tables of months and kalendar of saints. Similar kalendars are in the British Museum and the University Library, Cambridge. They were probably made early in the sixteenth century.

KRANTZ (ALBRECHT).   Chronica Regnorum Aquilonarium.
                              fol. *Johan Schott.   Strasburg*, 1548.
Title. CHRONICA | REGNORVM | AQVILONARIVM | DANIÆ SVETIAE | NORVAGIAE | Per Albertum Krantzium Ham- | burgen. descripta. | Cum Priuilegio CAESAREAE Maiestatis, | ad Quinquennium, iam recens edita, | sub annum Christi | M.D.XLVI. | ARGENT. apud Ioannem | Schottum.   Leaf 382ᵇ *Colophon.*   ☝ ARGENTORATI apud IOANNEM | Schottum. VIII. Kalend. Februarii. Anno | M.D.XLVIII.

Collation.   a⁴, b–z, aa–zz, Aaa–Ttt⁶ ; 388 leaves.   40 lines.   With headlines and numbers to pages.

Leaf 1ᵃ Title, 1ᵇ blank, 2ᵃ–3ᵃ Dedication, 3ᵇ–4ᵃ Lists of kings, 4ᵇ Woodcut of arms, 5 Prologue, 6ᵃ–382ᵇ Text, 383ᵃ–388ᵃ Index, 388ᵇ blank.
[*R.L.*]   [2213.]

LANGLAND (WILLIAM).   The vision of Piers Plowman.
                              4to.   *Robert Crowley.   London*, 1550.
Title [within border].   THE VISION | of Pierce Plowman, now | fyrste imprynted by Roberte | Crowley, dwellyng in Ely | rentes in Holburne. | Anno Domini. | ☙ | Cum priuilegio ad im- | primendū solum. | [Type ornaments.]   Leaf 127ᵇ *Colophon.*   ☝ Imprinted at London by Roberte | Crowley, dwellyng in Elye rentes | in Holburne.   The yere of | our Lord. M.D.L. | [Type ornaments].

Collation.   [2] *⁴, ☝⁴, A–Z, Aa–Ff⁴, Gg² ; 128 leaves.   32 lines.   With headlines and numbers to pages.

Leaf 1ᵃ Title, 1ᵇ blank, 2ᵃ The printer to the reader, 2ᵇ Prologe, 3ᵃ Second title, 3ᵇ blank, 4ᵃ Printer to the reader, 4ᵇ Prologe, 5ᵃ–10ᵃ Sum of principal points, 10ᵇ blank, 11ᵃ–127ᵇ Text, 128 blank. [*B.L.*]   [1302.]

The bibliography of this edition is rather confusing.   The genuine title-page of the first edition bears the date 1505.   When this mistake was noticed an ornament was stamped over the date, as in the present example, and later the real date 1550 was printed in small numerals below the ornament as in a Bodleian example.   Then a new title-page and pre-fatory matter were printed, which though asserting "nowe the seconde tyme imprinted" were added to all the unsold stock of the first issue, so that several copies like the present are known with two title-pages.   The genuine first issue of the text may be known from the misprinted signatures Tiij for Uiii and Fij for Ffij.   There is a re-issue of the "second edition" title-page and prefatory matter which reads on the title-page "nowe the seconde time," but it never occurs with the first issue of the text.

LE FEVRE (RAOUL).   The recuyles of the histories of Troy.

fol.   *Wynkyn de Worde.   London,* 1502.

Title [woodcut].   THE recuyles or gaderī | ge to gyder of yᵉ hysto- | ryes of Troye how it | was destroyed *&* brent | twyes by yᵉ puyssant | Hercules *&* yᵉ thyrde *&* | generall by yᵉ grekes.   Leaf 202ᵇ *Colophon.* ⊄ Thus endeth the boke of the recu- | les or syege of Troye.   Enprynted in | London in Flete strete at the sygne of | the sonne by wynkyn de worde. The | yere of our lorde god . M.CCCCC. | and . ij . | [W de Worde's device 4 within borders.]

Collation.   aa⁴, A–Z, Aa–Kk⁶ ; 202 leaves.   42 lines.   No headlines or numbers to pages.

Leaf 1ᵃ Title, 1ᵇ–4ᵇ Table, 5ᵃ–202ᵇ Text.   [*B.L.*]   **[1996.]**

Wants leaves 24, 92, 96, 167.

Editions of this book were issued by Wynkyn de Worde in 1502 and 1503, but it is probable that, beyond the date, they do not vary.   A copy formerly in the possession of Mr. Quaritch had the printed date 1503. The copy in the British Museum is imperfect at the end, and that in King's College, Cambridge, has the date altered to 1503 by hand.

LELAND (JOHN).   The laborious journey.

8°.   [*Richard Jugge.*]   *London,* 1549.

Title.   ⊄ The labo- | ryouse Iourney *&* serche | of Johan Leylande, for Englandes | Antiquitees, geuen of hym as a newe | yeares gyfte to Kynge Henry the | viii. in the . xxxvii . yeare of | his Reygne, with decla- | racyons enlarged : | by Johan Bale. | ii. Macha. ii.   [Text follows.]   ⊄ To be sold in fletestrete at the signe | of the Croune next vnto the whyte | Fryears gate.   Leaf 63ᵇ *Colophon.*   ⊄ Emprented at London by Johan | Bale, Anno. M.D.XLIX.

Collation. A–H⁸ ; 64 leaves. 27 lines. With headlines ; no numbers to pages.

Leaf 1ᵃ Title, 1ᵇ blank, 2ᵃ–6ᵃ Dedication, 6ᵇ–14ᵇ John Bale to the reader, 15ᵃ–63ᵇ Text. [*B.L.*]   [108.¹]

This copy wants the last leaf.

Though said in the colophon to have been printed by Bale, it is probable that he did nothing more than commission it. The type in which it is printed belonged to Richard Jugge, and the shop with the sign of the Crown next the Whitefriars gate in Fleet Street belonged to Richard Foster, the publisher of others of Bale's works.

LIDGATE (JOHN). The history, siege and destruction of Troy.
                        fol. *Richard Pynson. London,* 1513.

Title. The hystorye, Sege and dystruccyon of Troye. [Woodcut of Royal arms.] Leaf 162ᵇ *Colophon.* Here endeth the Troye booke | otherwyse called the Sege of | Troye, translated by Johñ Lyd | gate monke of the Monastery of | Bery, And Emprynted the yere | of oure Lorde a.M.CCCC. | &. xiii. by Richard Pynson, pryn- | ter vnto the kyngȝ noble grace. [Pynson's device.]

Collation. +², A–Z, A–C⁶, D⁴ ; 162 leaves. 50 lines. With headlines ; no numbers to pages.

Leaf 1ᵃ Title, 1ᵇ Woodcut, 2 Tabula, 3ᵃ–5ᵃ Prologue, 5ᵃ–162ᵇ Text. [*B.L.*]   [2257.]

Printed on vellum. Two other copies on vellum are known, one in the collection of Mr. A. H. Huth, the other at Bamburgh Castle.

This is one of the few books in the library retaining its original binding of leather over wooden boards.

—— The fall of princes and princesses.
                        fol. *Richard Tottell. London,* 1554.

Title [within border]. A TREATISE | excellent and compēdious, shewing | and declaring, in maner of Tragedye, the | falles of sondry most notable Princes and Princesses with o- | ther Nobles, through yᵉ mutabilitie and | change of vnstedfast Fortune together with their most | detestable & wicked vices. First com- | pyled in Latin by the excellent Clerke Bocati- | us, an Italian borne. And sence | that tyme translated into our | English and Uulgare tong, | by Dan John Lid- | gate Monke of Be | rye. And nowe newly im- | prynted, correc- | ted, and aug- | mented out | of diuerse and | sundry | olde writen copies | in parchment. | In ædibus Richardi Tottelli. | Cum priuilegio. Leaf 234^b *Colophon*. ⊄ Imprinted at London | in Fletestrete within Temple barre at | the sygne of the hande and starre, by Richard | Tottel, the .x. day of September in the | yeare of oure Lorde. | 1554. | Cum Priuilegio ad impri- | mendum solum.

Collation. ⊄, A–Y, Aa–Pp^6, ⊄⊄^{6} ; 234 leaves. 50 lines. With head-lines and numbers to pages.

Leaf 1^a Title, 1^b blank, 2^a–6^b Table, 7^a–9^b Prologue, 10^a–227^b Text, 228^a L'Envoy, 228^b blank, 229^a–234^b Daunce of Machabree. [*B.L.*]
[**2272.**]

LILY (WILLIAM).   De constructione octo partium orationis.
8°.   *Henry Pepwell.   London*, 1539.
Title [within border].   ☞ LIBELLVS | de Constructione | Octo partium | orationis. | LONDINI diligentia | Henrici Pepuuel, Ad | uerum Paulinæ | scholæ exem- | plum. | An M.D.XXXIX.   Leaf 20^b *Colophon*. ✍ Explicit Libellus de Constructione Octo par- | tium orationis.   Londini Impressus per Henricum | Pepuuel, in cemiterio diui Pauli. Anno a partu | uirgineo M.D.XXXIX.

Collation.   AB^8, C^4 ; 20 leaves. 29 lines. With headlines ; no numbers to pages.

Leaf 1^a Title, 1^b Colet to Lily, 2^a–20^b Text. [*R.T.*]   [**424^7.**]

The title is within the same border as is used in Colet's Paul's Accidence [424^5]. In spite of the assertion in the title and colophon it is clear that this book was printed at Antwerp.

Bibliographica I. 187. The only copy known.

——— De generibus nominum.   8°. *Martin de Keyser. Antwerp*, 1535.
Title [within border].   ☜ GVILI- | HELMI LILII | GRAMMATICI & POE- | tæ eximij, Paulinæ scholæ olim | moderatoris, De generibus no | minum, ac uerborum præte | ritis & supinis, Regu- | læ pueris apprime | utiles. | ☞ OPVS RECOGNITVM | & adauctum, cum nominum ac uer- | borum interpretamentis, per Ioan - | nem Rituissum, scholæ Paulinæ | præceptorem.   Leaf 28^a *Colophon*.   EXCVDEBAT ANTVERPIAE | Martinus Cæsar . Anno a Christo | nato Millesimo, Quingen - | tesimo. Trigesimo | Quinto.

Collation.   A–C^8, D^4 ; 28 leaves. 26 lines. No headlines or numbers to pages.

Leaf 1^a Title, 1^b-2^a Prefatory verses, 2^b-28^a Text, 28^b blank. [*Ital.*] [**424^3.**]

LILY (WILLIAM).   De generibus nominum.

8°.   *Henry Pepwell.   London,* 1539.

Title.   GVILI- | ELMI LILII GRAMMA | tici & poetæ eximii, Paulinæ | scholæ olim moderatoris | De generibus nominum, | ac uerborum præte | ritis & supinis. | Regulæ pueris apprime utiles. | Opus recognitum & adactum | cum Nominum, ac Verbo | rum interprætamentis. | An. M.D.XXXIX.   Leaf 24ᵇ *Colophon.*   EXCVSVM Londini in Cimiterio diui | pauli, per me Henricum Pepuuel, Anno a | partu uirgineo. M.D.XXXIX.

Collation. a–c⁸ ; 24 leaves.   30 lines.   No headlines or numbers to pages.
Leaf 1ᵃ Title, 1ᵇ blank, 2 Prefatory verses, 3ᵃ–24ᵇ Text.   [424⁸.]
Bibliographica I. 186.   The only copy known.

LITURGIES.   Church of England.

BOOK OF COMMON PRAYER. fol. *Richard Grafton.   London,* 1549.
Title [within border].   THE | booke of the common praier | and administracion of the | Sacramentes, and | other rites and | ceremonies | of the | Churche : after the | vse of the Churche of | Englande. | LONDINI, in officina Richardi Graftoni, | Regii impressoris. | Cum priuilegio ad imprimendum solum. | Anno Domini. M.D.XLIX | Mense Martij.

Collation.   ¹⁰, A–R⁸, ST⁶ ; 158 leaves.   37 lines.   With headlines ; no numbers to pages.

Leaf 1ᵃ Title, 1ᵇ Contents, 2 Preface, 3ᵃ–10ᵃ Psalms and lessons, 10ᵇ blank, 11ᵃ–158ᵇ Text. [*B.L.*]   [1976¹.]
Wants last leaf.

——, noted. [by John Marbeck]. 4to. *Richard Grafton.   London,* 1550.

Title [within borders].   The booke | of Common | praier noted. | | 1550.   Leaf 68ᵇ *Colophon.*   [Printer's device.] | IMPRINTED BY RICHARD | GRAFTON PRINTER TO THE | KINGES MAIESTIE. | 1550 | Cum priuilegio ad imprimendum solum.

Collation. A², B–R⁴, S² ; 68 leaves.   With headlines ; no numbers to pages.
Leaf 1ᵃ Title, 1ᵇ blank, 2ᵃ Contents and notes on music, 2ᵇ blank, 3ᵃ–68ᵃ Text, 68ᵇ colophon. [*B.L.*]   [1118.]
With five pages of MS. music at end.

Liturgies : Church of England.

DEVOUT PSALMS.   8°.   *Edward Whitchurch.   London* [1550.]

Title [within border].   Deuout psalmes | and collectes, gathered | and set in suche | order, as may be | vsed for daylye | meditacions.   Leaf 56^b *Colophon.* ℂ Imprinted at London | in flete strete at the sygne of the sunne, | by Edward Whitchurche. | Cum priuilegio ad imprimen- | dum solum.

Collation. A–G^8 ; 56 leaves. 22 lines. With headlines ; no numbers to pages.

Leaf 1^a Title, 1^b blank, 2^a–3^b Exhortation to prayer, 4^a–45^b Psalms, etc., 46^a–56^b Litany, Lord's prayer, twelve articles, etc. [*B.L.*]   [75^1.]

ORDER OF St BARTHOLOMEW'S HOSPITAL.

                              8°.   *Richard Grafton.   London,* 1552.

Title.   The ordre of | the Hospital of S. Bar- | tholomewes in west- | smythfielde in | London. | ℂ i Epist. Ihon. ij. Chap. | He that sayeth he walketh in the lyght, and hateth his | brother, came neuer as yeat in the lyght.   But | he that loueth his brother, he dwel- | leth in the lyght. | LONDONI. | ANNO | 1552.   Leaf 72^a *Colophon.*   Imprinted at London by Ry- | charde Grafton, Printer to the | Kynges maiestie. | Cum priuilegio ad imprimen- | dum solum.   ✓

Collation. A–I^8 ; 72 leaves. 22 lines. With headlines ; no numbers to pages.

Leaf 1^a Title, 1^b Contents, 2^a–8^a Preface, 8^b blank, 9^a–45^a The order of the hospital, 45^b blank, 46^a–64^b Service for the poor, 65^a–69^b Litany and suffrages, 70^a–71^a a prayer, 71^b–72^a A passport for the poor, 72^b blank. [*B.L.*]   [138.]

————

Title.   The Order | Of the | Hospitalls of K. Henry | the viijth and K. Ed- | ward the vith, | viz. St. Bartholomew's. | Christ's. | Bridewell. | St. Thomas's. | By the Maior, Cominaltie, and Ci- | tizens of London, Gouernours of | the Possessions, Revenues and | Goods of the sayd Hospitalls, | 1557.

Collation.   [A]^4, B–H^8 ; 60 leaves. 22 lines. With headlines ; no numbers to pages.

Leaf 1 blank, 2^a Title, 2^b blank, 3^a–4^a Offley Major, 4^b blank, 5^a–59^a Order of the Hospitalls, 59^b, 60 blank. [*B.L.*]   [394.]

A seventeenth century reprint.

Liturgies: Church of England.

PRAYER FOR VICTORY.   8°.   *Richard Grafton.*   *London,* 1548.

Title. ✠ A PRA- | YER FOR | VICTO- | RIE | AND | PEACE. Leaf 6^b *Colophon.* EXCVSVM | LONDINI, IN | AEDIBVS RI- | CHARDI GRAF- | TONI, TYPOGRA- | PHI REGII. | Anno salutis humanæ. | M.D.XLVIII. | CVM PRIVILEGIO | AD IMPRIMEN- | DVM SOLVM.

Collation. A^8; 8 leaves.   17 lines.   With headlines; no numbers to pages.

Leaf 1^a Title, 1^b blank, 2^a–6^a Prayer, 6^b Colophon, 7^a Grafton's device, 7^b, 8 blank.   [*B.L.*]   **[1976^2.]**

THANKSGIVING.   8°.   *Richard Grafton.*   *London,* 1551.

Title [within borders].   A thankes | geuing to God | vsed in Christes | churche on the | Mon- | day | Wednisday | and Friday. | 1551. | Richardus Grafton | excudebat | Mense Iulij.   Ends leaf 12^a.   For it is we o lord, that haue offended, | deale therfore fauorably with vs o mer | ciful god, and we wil bewaile our | offences and blesse and praise | thy holy name, bothe nowe | and for euer | Amen. | R G.

Collation. A^8, B^4; 12 leaves.   25 lines.   With headlines; no numbers to pages.

Leaf 1^a Title, 1^b blank, 2^a–12^a Text, 12^b Grafton's device.   [*B.L.*]
                                         [228^2.]

Church of Rome.   Diocese of Le Mans.

HORAE.   Heures a l'usage de Mans.   8°.   *for Simon Vostre.*   *Paris* [1515.]

Title [within borders].   [Device of Simon Vostre] | ◖ Ces presentes heures a lusaige du Mans toutes | au long sans reqrir : auec les figures & signes de lapo | calipse : la vie de thobie & de iudic, les accidēs de lhō | me, le triumphe de cesar, les miracles nostre dame : | ont este faictes a Paris pour symō Uostre libraire | demourāt en la rue neufue a lēseigne . s . iehā leuāgel.   Ends leaf 140^b.   hoc templum beneficia petiturus in- | gredit̃ cūcta se ĩpetrasse letetur.   Per. | Deo gratias.

Collation. a–c^8, d^4, e–n^8, A–E^8; 140 leaves.   21-22 lines.   No headlines or numbers to pages.

Liturgies : Church of Rome, diocese of Le Mans.

Leaf 1ᵃ Title, 1ᵇ Almanack, 2ᵃ Anatomical man, 2ᵇ–8ᵃ Kalendar, 8ᵇ Woodcut, 9°–140ᵇ Text. [*B.L.*]   [993.]

Contains seventeen large woodcuts, and each page is surrounded by borders. One woodcut, differing in style from the rest, is signed F. G.

This copy is on vellum.

Church of Rome.   Diocese of Salisbury.

BREVIARIUM AD USUM SARUM.
P.H.   4to.   *John Kingston and Henry Sutton.   London,* 1555.
P.E.   4to.   *Robert Caly.   London,* 1555.

Title [within borders]. ℂ Portiforium | seu Breuiarium, ad insignis | Sarisburiensis, ecclesie vsum : accu- | ratissime castigatum, cum multis | annotaciūculis ac litteris Al- | phabeticis, Euangeliorum | & Epistolarum, capitulo- | rumq3 originem indi- | cantibus : que nusq̄, | hucusq3 fuerunt | addite. | ℂ Pars hyemalis. | Impress. Londini. | 1555. | Leaf 281ᵇ *Colophon.* ℂ Breuiarium seu Porti- | forium ad vsum ecclesie Sarisburiensis. | Londini impressum, Per Johannes Kyngston . | et Henricus Sutton typographi. Anno | dn̄i Millesimo quingētesimo quin- | quagesimo quinto . Die . ve- | ro septima mensis | Martii. | [Registrum etc.].

Collation. +¹⁰, A–O⁸, P⁴, a–o⁸, p⁴, A–E⁸ ; 282 leaves. 40 lines. With headlines and numbers to pages.

Leaf 1ᵃ Title, 1ᵇ blank, 2ᵃ–7ᵇ Kalendar, 8 Table of moveable feasts, 9, 10 Benedictio aquae et panis, 11ᵃ–126ᵇ De Tempore, 127ᵃ–242ᵇ Psalter and Commune, 243ᵃ–281ᵃ Proprium de sanctis, 281ᵇ colophon, 282 blank. [*B.L.*]   [1748.]

This copy wants leaves 132, 133, 197, 198, 242.

—— P.E.

Title [within borders]. Portiforiū seu | Breuiarium ad vsum ecclesie | Sarisburiensis castigatum, supple- | tum, marginalibus quotationibus | adornatum, ac nunc primum ad verissimum ordinalis exem- | plar in suum ordinem a | peritissimis viris re- | dactum. Pars | Estiualis . | Londini . | 1555. Leaf 339ᵇ *Colophon.* ℂ Pars estiualis tam de tēpore, q̄7 | de sanctis portifarii ad vsu3 insig- | nis ecclesie Sa ꝩ optimis formulis | (vt res ipsa ĩdicat) diligentissime re | uisum ac correctū. Et si quid in pri | oribus omissu3, aut in aliquo erra- | tu3 fuit appositū siue emēdatum est | in alma

Liturgies: Church of Rome, diocese of Salisbury.

vniuersitate . Parisieñ . im- | pressa p . Franciscū regnault . Anno | domini Millesimo quingentesimo | trigesimo quinto. | [Registrum].

Collation. ‡⁸, A–D, ²D, ³D, EF⁴, a–r⁸, s⁴, aa–qq⁸ ; 340 leaves. 37 lines. With headlines ; no numbers to pages.

Leaf 1ᵃ Title, 1ᵇ blank, 2ᵃ–7ᵇ Kalendar, 8 Compotus, 9, 10 Pica, 11ᵃ–72ᵇ De Tempore, 73ᵃ–212ᵇ Psalterium *&* Commune, 213ᵃ Title, 213ᵇ–339ᵇ Proprium Sanctorum, 340 blank. [*B.L.*]   [**1749.**]

HORAE AD USUM SARUM.   4to.   *Francis Regnault.   Paris,* 1530.

Title [within borders].   ℂ Hore Beatissime vir | ginis marie ad legitimum Sarisburiensis Eccle | sie ritum, cum quindecim orationibus beate Bri- | gitte, ac multis aliis orationibus pulcherrimis, | et indulgentiis, cum tabula aptissima iam vltimo | adiectis.   1530 | [Woodcut.] | ℂ Uenundantur Parisiis a Francisco Regnault | In vico sancti Jacobi, sub signo Elephantis. Leaf 204ᵃ *Colophon.* ℂ Hore beatissime virginis Marie, secundū vsum | Sarisbu. totaliter ad lōgum, cum multis pul- | cherrimis orationibus et indulgētiis iam | vltimo adiectis.   Impresse Parisii | per Franciscum Regnault alme | vniuersitatis parisiensis li | brarium iuratum. | Impensis et | sumpti- | bus | eiusdem.

Collation.   +¹⁰, A–Z⁸, *&*¹⁰ ; 204 leaves. 30 lines. With headlines and numbers to pages.

Leaf 1ᵃ Title, 1ᵇ Woodcut and Salutation, 2ᵃ–7ᵇ Kalendar, 8ᵃ–10ᵇ Tables, etc., 11ᵃ–200ᵇ Text, 201ᵃ–204ᵃ Table, 204ᵇ Device.   [**1848.**]

This copy wants the first three and last eleven leaves, which have been supplied in illuminated manuscript.

Every page is surrounded by elaborate engraved borders, many evidently intended for use in English service books containing the Royal arms, a shield with three roses and pictures of St. George and St. Edward. The book is also fully illustrated, some of the larger engravings having the engraver's mark L.V.

PRIMER.   Prymer of Salysbury use.   16°.   *Yolande Bonhomme, widow of Thielman Kerver, for John Growte (London).   Paris,* 1532.
Title.   ℂ This prymer of Salysbury vse is set | out a long wout ony serchyng, with | many prayers, and goodly pyctures in | the kalendar, in the matyns of our lady, | in the houres of the crosse, in the . VII . | psalmes, *&* in the dyryge.   And be newly | enprynted at Parys. | [Device

Liturgies : Church of Rome, diocese of Salisbury.

of Thielman Kerver] M.D.xxxii. Leaf 288ᵃ *Colophon.* ℂ Expliciunt
hore beatissime virginis | Marie secūdum vsum Sarum, totaliter | ad
longum, cum orationibus beate Bri- | gitte, ac multis aliis, impresse
Parisiis, | impensis quidem honesti viri Joannis | Growte, librarii, opera
autem cōspicue | matrone yolande Bonhomme vidua | defuncti Thielmanni
Kerver, sub vni- | corni commorātis, in vico diui Jacobi. | Anno dn̄i.
M.D.xxxii. | mense Augusto. 288ᵇ [Kerver's device] M.D.xxxii.

Collation. a–z, A–N⁸ ; 288 leaves. 23 lines. With headlines and
numbers to pages.

Leaf 1ᵃ Title, 1ᵇ–7ᵃ Changes of the Moon, 7ᵇ Almanack, 1532–48, 8ᵃ
To find Easter, 8ᵇ–26ᵃ Kalendar, 26ᵇ–27ᵇ Rhymes on the week days,
28ᵃ–287ᵇ Text, 288ᵃ Colophon, 288ᵇ Device and date. [*B.L.*]   [23¹.]

PRIMER.

Title. ℂ A goodly prymer in englyshe, newly corrected and prin | ted,
with certeyne godly meditations and prayers | added to the same, very
necessarie & profitable | for all them that ryghte assuredly vnder | stande
not yᵉ latine & greke tongues. | [Woodcut of arms H. A.] ℂ with the
kyngᵍ most gracious priuilege for . vi . yeres. Leaf 169ᵇ. ℂ Imprynted at
London in Fletestrete by | John̄ Byddell, dwellynge at the signe | of the
Sonne, nexte to the cundite, | for wylliam Marshall, the | yere of our lorde
god | M.D.xxxv. the | xvi. day of | June.

Collation. [1] A–F, A–R, A–T⁴ ; 169 leaves. 32 lines. With headlines ; no numbers to pages.

Leaf 1ᵃ Title, 1ᵇ Woodcut, 2ᵃ–6ᵃ Admonition, 6ᵇ Almanack, 7ᵃ–12ᵇ
Kalendar, 13ᵃ–14ᵃ Preface, 14ᵇ–168ᵇ Text, 169ᵃ Table, 169ᵇ Colophon.

This copy wants the title-page.   [1374¹.]

HORAE.   4to. *John Wayland. London,* 1539.

Title [within border]. ℂ The Manual of prayers | or the prymer in
Englysh & | Laten set out at length, whose con- | tentes the reader by yᵉ
prologe next | after the Kalēder, shal sone per- | ceaue, and there in shall
se | brefly the order of the | whole boke. | [Two texts.] | ℂ Set forth by
Ihon by Goddes | grace & the Kynges callying, Bys- | shoppe of Rochester
at the cōmaun | demente of the ryghte honorable lorde Thomas | Crumwell,
lorde Priuie seale, Uicegerent to the | Kynges hyghnes. Leaf 196ᵇ
Colophon. ℂ Imprinted at Lōdō in fletestrete by me John̄ | Wayland in

Liturgies : Church of Rome, diocese of Salisbury.

saynt Dūstones parysh at the signe | of the blew Garland next to the Temple | bare. In the yere of our Lorde God | a M.D.xxxix. the | xv daye of July. | Cum priuilegio ad Impri- | mendum solum.

Collation. A⁴, A, BB–DD⁴, EE², A–Z, Aa–Ii⁴, +², Kk–Vv⁴ ; 196 leaves.

Leaf 1ᵃ Title, 1ᵇ–2ᵃ Bishop of Rochester to Crumwell, 2ᵇ–8ᵃ Kalendar, 8ᵇ–10ᵃ Prologue, 10ᵃ–196ᵇ Text.　　　　　**[1403.]**

Wants leaves 103, 150, 190, 191, partly supplied in MS.

MANUALE ad usum percelebris ecclesie Sarisburiensis.
　　　　　4to. [*John Kingston and Henry Sutton.*] *London,* 1554.
Title [within border]. ❧ Manuale ad | vsum per celebris eccle- | sie Sarisburiensis. | Londini recenter im- | pressū, necnō mul- | tis mendis ter- | sum atq̄, emū- | datum. | Londini. | Anno Domini. | 1554. Leaf 168ᵃ *Colophon.* ❧ Explicit Manuale ad | vsum insignis ecclesie Sarisburiensis tam | in cantu q̄, in litera diligentissime re- | cognitum : et nusq̄, ante hac eli- | matius impressum. In quo ea | que seruat ecclesiasticus ri- | tus ordine congruo | connectuntur. | LONDINI, | 1554.

Collation. a–x⁸ ; 168 leaves. 32 lines. With headlines and numbers to pages.

Leaf 1ᵃ Title, 1ᵇ blank, 2ᵃ–167ᵃ Text, 167ᵇ–168ᵃ Table, 168ᵇ blank.
[*B.L.*]　　　　　**[1699.]**

MISSALE AD USUM SARUM. fol. *Richard Pynson. London,* 1520.
Title [within a border]. ⊄ Missale ad vsum insignis ac pre- | clare ecclesie Sarum. | [Woodcut of Royal arms.] Qui diuina cupit summo libamina patri | Donaq̄, sublimi mystica ferre deo | Hec legat a terra purgata volumine labe | Num prestant faciles ad pia sacra vias | Horum presidio mysteria Sancta parabit | Et celi dn̄o munera grata feret. Leaf 200ᵇ *Colophon.* ⊄ In laudē sctissime trinitatis totiusq̄, | militie celestis ac honorē et decorē sancte | ecclesie Sarū Anglicane : eiusq̄, deuotis- | simi cleri : hoc missale diuinorū officiorū | vigilanti studio emendatū et reuisum. | Impressum Londini . Per Richardum | Pynson . in fletestrete apud diuū dunsta | num cōmorantem . Anno dn̄i M.D.xx | nono kalendas Januarii . felici numine | explicitum est. | ⊄ Cum gratia et priuilegio.

Collation. +⁸, A–L⁶, M⁸, N⁴, O–R⁶, S⁸, a–l⁶, A–Æ⁶ F⁸ ; 202 leaves. 50 lines. With headlines and numbers to pages.

Liturgies : Church of Rome, diocese of Salisbury.

Leaf 1ᵃ Title, 1ᵇ Speculum sacerdotum, 2ᵃ–7ᵇ Kalendar, 8ᵃ–9ᵃ Bendictio salis et aque, etc., 9ᵇ Woodcut of Royal arms, 10ᵃ–110ᵇ Temporale, 111ᵃ–164ᵇ Sanctorale, 165ᵃ–200ᵇ Commune Sanctorum, 201ᵃ–202ᵇ Cautele missae and Tabula. [*B.L. Red and Black.*] **[2795.]**

Printed on vellum.

This is perhaps the finest production of the early English press and is a marvel of taste and typographical skill.

ORDINALE SARUM.   4to.   *Richard Pynson.   London,* 1503.

Title. ¶ Ordinale Sarum.   Leaf 209ᵇ *Colophon.*   ¶ Exaratum est presens opus per me | Ricardum pynson cōmorātē in flete- | strete Londoñ ad intersigniū sancti | Georgii Iuxta eccl'iam scti Dūstani. | Finit feliciter. Ano dñi M.d. iii. die ve | ro vltima mensis Augusti.

Collation.   aa⁸, a³, cd⁶, ef⁸, gh⁶, i⁸, kl⁶, m⁸, no⁶, p⁸, qz⁶, &⁶, 2⁶, A–G⁶, H⁴ ; 210 leaves.   31 lines.   With headlines ; no numbers to pages.

Leaf 1ᵃ Title, 1ᵇ Animadvertendum, 2ᵃ–7ᵇ Kalendar, 8ᵃ blank, 8ᵇ Almanack, 9ᵃ–10ᵃ Prologus, 10ᵇ Numbers, 11ᵃ–209ᵇ Text, 210ᵃ blank, 210ᵇ Pynson's device 3.   [*B.L.*]   **[1700.]**

The only other copy known is in the Bodleian.   A copy was sold in Richard Smith's sale in 1682.

PROCESSIONALE AD USUM SARUM.
          4to.   [*John Kingston and Henry Sutton.*]   *London,* 1554.

Title [within border].   Processionale | ad vsum insignis eccl'ie Saʑ, | obseruandos accommodum preser- | tim in iisque in habendis processio- | nibus, ad ceremoniarum splendo- | rem faciunt imprimis opportu- | num : iam denuo ad calculos | reuocatū : et a multis qui- | bus ipsum viciatum e- | rat mendis, purga- | tum atq̢ ter- | sum .·. | 🍶 | Impressum Lond. | 1554.   Leaf 195ᵃ *Colophon.*   ¶ Explicit Processionale ad vsus [*sic*] insignis | Ecclesie Sarum obseruandos ac- | cōmodum : iterum prelo ap- | plicatum absolutūq̢. | LONDINI, | Anno Domini. M.D.LIIII.

Collation.   a–z, A⁸ B⁴ ; 196 leaves.   With headlines and numbers to pages.

Leaf 1ᵃ Title, 1ᵇ blank, 2ᵃ–193ᵇ Text, 194ᵃ–195ᵃ Index, 195ᵇ, 196 blank. [*B.L.*]   **[1238.]**

Liturgies : Church of Rome, diocese of Salisbury.

PSALTER OF JESUS.   16°.   [*Paris.*] [1532.]

Leaf 1ᵃ.   ℂ An inuocacyon gloryous | named the psalter of Jesus.
Leaf 16ᵇ ends, after theyr power, that god the rather | maye lyghten theyr
hertis, & the soner tur | ne to goodnes. | ℂ Finis.

Collation. +, ++⁸ ; 16 leaves. 25 lines. No headlines or numbers
to pages. [*B.L.*]   [23¹.]

This little book, though with separate signatures, was issued without title,
as it was intended as a supplement to the Horae ad usum Sarum.

PSALTERIUM AD USUM SARUM.
          8°.   *John Kyngston and Henry Sutton.   London,* 1555.

Title [within borders].   ℂ Psal- | terium Dauidi- | cum, ad vsum eccle- |
sie Sarisburiensis. | ◆ Impressum | Londini, per Ioannem | Kyngston, &
Hen- | ricum Sutton, | Typogra- | phos. | 1555. Ends leaf 144ᵃ. Uoce
mea ad dominum cla . ii . cxli.

Collation. [8], A–R⁸ ; 144 leaves. 24 lines. No headlines or numbers
to pages.

Leaf 1ᵃ Title, 1ᵇ blank, 2ᵃ–7ᵇ Kalendar, 8ᵃ Almanack, 8ᵇ blank, 9ᵃ–140ᵇ
Text, 141ᵃ–144ᵃ Index, 144ᵇ blank. [*B.L.*]   [301.]

Church of Rome.   Diocese of York.

HORAE AD USUM EBOR.   8°.   *for John Wight.   London* [1556.]

Title [within border].   ℂ Hore beate | Marie virginis, | secundum
vsum | insignis ec- | clesie Eboriensis. | de nouo Impres. | ℂ Imprinted at
Lon- | don for Ihon | Wight. Ends leaf 80ᵇ. Dulcissime domine da michi
mun- | duȝ, contritū, q̄etū, patiens et humi | le castum corpus obediens et
sta- | bile semper in tuis obsequiis manci- | putum . Qui viuis. | FINIS.

Collation. A–K⁸ ; 80 leaves. 21 lines. No headlines or numbers to
pages.

Leaf 1ᵃ Title, 1ᵇ–4ᵃ Kalendar, 4ᵇ–80ᵇ Text.   [136.]

The only copy known. Some fragments are in the library of York
Minster.

Liturgies : Church of Rome, diocese of York.

MANUALE INSIGNIS ECCLESIAE EBORACENSIS.
4to.   *Wynkyn de Worde.   London,* 1509.

Title.   Ad laudem dei et honorē tuāq̆, non im | merito flos virgo maria
ecce manuale | quoddam secunduȝ usū matris eccl'ie | Eboraceñ . [*etc.*].
Leaf 103ᵇ *Colophon.*   ℂ Manuale insignis eccl'ie Eboraceñ . Impres- | sum
Per wynandū de worde cōmorātē iondoñ. | in vico nūcupato fletestrete sub
Intersignio so- | lis : vel in cimiterio sancti pauli sub ymagine di | ue marie
pietatis . (pro Johāñe gaschet et Jaco- | bo ferrebouc sociis) Finit . Anno
dñi millesimo | quīgētesimo nono quarto ydus Februarii. | Sane hoc
volumen digessit arte magister | wynandus de worde incola londonii.

Collation.   a–nᵇ ; 104 leaves.   29 lines.   With headlines ; no numbers
to pages.

Leaf 1ᵃ Title, 1ᵇ blank, 2ᵃ–103ᵇ Text.   [*B.L.*]   [**1823.**]

Although the colophon states distinctly that the book was printed by
Wynkyn de Worde, it seems fairly certain that it is the work of a foreign
press.   The types both of text and music are not De Worde's, and the two
curious woodcuts which occur in it are from the set used in " The Passion
of our Lord " printed abroad about the same time.

MALORY (SIR THOMAS).   La morte d'Arthur.
fol.   *William Copland.   London,* 1557.

Title.   The Story of the moste noble and worthy Kynge Arthur, the
whyche was the fyrst of the worthyes chrysten, and also of his noble
and valyaunt knyghtes of the rounde Table.   Newly imprynted and
corrected.

Leaf 310ᵇ *Colophon.*   ℂ Imprynted at Londō in Fletestrete | at the sygne
of the Rose Gar | lande, by Wyllyam | Copland. | [Border piece.] |

Collation.   +⁶₊⁸, a–d⁸, e⁸, (+⁴ *)⁹, f–z, A–o⁸ ; 311 leaves.   44 lines.
With headlines ; no numbers to pages.

Leaf 1ᵃ Title, 2ᵃ–3ᵇ Prologue, 3ᵇ–14ᵃ Table, 14ᵇ blank, 15ᵃ–310ᵇ Text,
311 Device.   [**1982.**]

Title-page wanting and last leaf.   The only perfect copy known was in
the Huth Library.

MARCORT (ANTHONY).   A declaration of the mass.

8°.   Hans Luft.   Wittenberg, 1547.

Title. ❧ A declarati | on of the masse, the fruyte | therof the cause
& the mea- | ne, wherfore and howe it oughte | to be maynteyned. |
℘ Newly perused and augmented | by the fyrst author therof. | Mayster
Anthony Mar- | cort at Geneue. | Johan. vi. | ℘ I am the bread of lyfe,
who so cometh | to me shall haue no hunger.   And | who that beleueth in
me | shall neuer haue | thurste. | Translated newly out of Frenche | into
Englysshe.   Anno | M.D.XLUII.   Leaf 31ᵇ *Colophon.*   MDXLUII. |
℘ Prynted at Wyttenberge | by Hans Luft.

Collation.   A–Dˢ ; 32 leaves.   36 lines.   No headlines or numbers to
pages.

Leaf 1ᵃ Title, 1ᵇ C. Geranius to the reader, 2ᵃ–5ᵇ Preface, 5ᵇ–31ᵇ Text,
32 blank.   [209².]

There are two different editions of this book with the same colophon.
Copies of both are in the Cambridge University Library.

Leaf 32 wanting.

MEDINA (PEDRO DE).   L'art de naviguer.

fol.   Guillaume Roville.   Lyons, 1552.

Title [within border].   L'ART DE NAVIGVER | DE MAISTRE
PIERRE DE ME- | dine, Espaignol : contenant toutes les | reigles, secrets,
& enseignemens | necessaires, à la bonne | nauigation. | TRADUICT
DE CASTIL- | lan en François, auec augmentation & illustration | de
plusieurs figures & annotations, par Ni- | colas de Nicolai, du Dauphiné,
Geo- | graphe du tres-Chrestien Roy | HENRI II. DE | CE NOM : | Et
dedié a sa tres-Augu- | ste Maiesté. | A LYON. | CHEZ GVILLAVME |
ROVILLE. | Auec Priuilege pour dix ans. | 1554.

Collation.   *⁶, a–z, A–F⁴ ; 122 leaves.   39 lines.   With headlines and
numbers to pages.

Leaf 1ᵃ Title, 1ᵇ Privilege, 2 Dedication of N de Nicolai to Henri II,
3ᵃ–4ᵃ Proeme, 4ᵇ–6ᵇ Table, 7ᵃ–121ᵃ Text, 121ᵇ, 122 blank.   [*R.L.*]   [**2455.**]

With woodcuts and diagrams.   Between leaves 15 and 16 is a fine map
of the world engraved by Nicolay.

MIRK (JOHN).   Liber festivalis.   fol.   *Richard Pynson.*   [*London,* 1493.]

Leaf 2ᵃ.   ℘ The helpe and grace of al- | mighty god thrugh the besech- |
inge of his blessed modre saynt | mary be with vs at oure begyn | nynge,
help vs and spede vs he | re in oure lyuynge and bringe | vs vnto the blisse

F

y^t neuir shalle | haue endynge . Amen . [*etc.*]   Leaf 92^b, col. 2, line 30 : on nyghtes whan they be buryed in ho | ly place but that is nat longe of the fē | de but of the grace of almyghty god. | whiche grace . he graunte vs all that | for vs shedde his blode on the rode tree | Amen : | ℂ Per me Ricardum Pynson.

Collation. a–d^8, e–h^6, i–m^8, n^4 ; 92 leaves.   40 lines.   No headlines or numbers to pages.

Leaf 1 not known, probably blank, 2^a–92^b Text.   [*B.L.*]   [1944^1.]

Wants leaves 1, 50, 56, 71.

The only copy known.   This edition does not contain the Nova Festa. A reprint by Pynson of almost the same date has the Nova Festa added as a supplement at the end.   In the edition printed by Wynkyn de Worde in 1493 they are incorporated in the text in their proper places.

MORE (SIR THOMAS). Works.
   fol. 1 vol. in 2. *John Cawood for J. Walley and R. Tottell.   London*, 1557.
   Title [within border].   ✿ THE | vvorkes of Sir | Thomas More Knyght, sometyme | Lorde Chauncellour of England, | wrytten by him in the En- | glysh tonge. | ✿ Printed at | London at the costes and charges | of Iohn Cawod, Iohn VValy, | and Richarde Tottell. | Anno. 1557. | [Cawood's mark.] Leaf 743^b *Colophon.*   ✿ Imprinted at Lon | don in Fletestrete at the sygne of the | hande and starre, at the coste and charge of | Iohn Cawod, Iohn Walley, and | Richarde Tottle. | Finished in Apryll, in the yere | of our Lorde God. 1557. | (∴) | ¶ Cum priuilegio ad impri- | mendum solum.

Collation.   ℂ^{10}, ℂ^8, a–e, (fg), h–z, aa–zz, A–Z, AA–YY^8, ZZ^6 ; 744 leaves.   60 lines.   With headlines and numbers to pages.

Leaf 1^a Title, 1^b blank, 2 William Rastell's dedication to Queen Mary, 3^a–9^b Tables, 10 blank (cancelled), 11^a–18^b Youthful works, 19^a–743^b Works, 744 blank.   [*B.L.*]   [2008–9.]

Wants leaf 744.

——   The debellacyon of Salem and Bizance.
                    8°.   *William Rastell.   London*, 1533.
   Title [within border].   The debella- | cyon of Sa- | lem and | Bizance. Leaf 277^b *Colophon.*   ℂ Prynted by w. Rastell in | Fletestrete in saynte | Bridys chyrch | yarde, the | yere | of | our lorde. | 1533. | Cum priuilegio. ∴

Collation.   a–n, A–Y^8; 280 leaves.   24 lines.   With headlines and numbers to pages.

Leaf 1ª Title, 1ᵇ–2ª The declaration of the title, 2ᵇ–7ᵇ Preface, 8ª–277ª Text, 277ᵇ Colophon, 278ª–279ᵇ Faults escaped. [*B.L.*]   [**752**².]

Some copies have at the end two extra leaves "Syr Thomas More to the chrysten reader." This was the last of the series of four controversial works written by More and Christopher Saint Germain, a celebrated lawyer. St. Germain published a book entitled "A treatise concerning the division between the temporalty and the spiritualty" which was answered by More in his "Apology." St. Germain followed with his "Dialogue of Salem and Bizance," to which the present book was an answer.

OCKHAM (WILLIAM OF).   A dialogue between a knight and a clerk.
8°.   *Thomas Berthelet.   London.*

Title [within border].   A DIALOGVE | betwene a knyght | and a clerke, | concer- | nynge the power spi- | ritual and tem- | porall. | ·🖙·. Leaf 26ᵇ *Colophon.*   ⊄ Imprinted at London in Flete- | strete, in the house of Thomas | Berthelet, nere to the cun | dite at the sygne of | Lucrece. | CVM PRIVILEGIO.

Collation.   A, B⁸, C¹⁰ ; 26 leaves.   24 lines.   With headlines and numbers to pages.

Leaf 1ª Title, 1ᵇ blank, 2ª–26ᵇ Text.   [*B.L.*]   [**368**².]

OF THE OLD GOD AND THE NEW.
8°.   *John Byddell.   London,* 1534.

Leaf 1ª [within borders].   A worke entytled of yᵉ | olde god & the newe, | of the olde faythe & the newe, | of the olde doctryne and | yᵉ newe, or orygynall | begynnynge of | Idolatrye. | [*etc.*].   Leaf 136ᵇ *Colophon.* Imprynted at London in | Fletestrete | by me Iohan | Byddell, dwelling | at yᵉ sygne of our Lady | of pite, next to Flete brydge . | M . v . C.xxxiiii . yᵉ xv. day of June | Cum priuilegio Regali. | Fyrste reade, and then Judge.

Collation.   A–R⁸ ; 136 leaves.   23 lines.   No headlines or numbers to pages.

Leaf 1ª Title and address to reader, 1ᵇ–8ᵇ Introduction, 9ª–13ᵇ Preface, 14ª–136ª Text, 136ᵇ colophon. [*B.L.*]   [**60.**]

The original of this work was published as early as 1521, and by 1523 at least six editions had been issued.   It was entitled "Vom alten und newen Gott : Glauben und Lere," and contains no author's name, though ascribed by Weller to Paulus Elias, a Carmelite.   In 1522–3 it was translated into Latin by Hartmannus Dulichius, because, as he remarks in his quaint preface, "sunt enim quos latina magis delectant, et vernacula, veluti levioris momenti, sordeant." The preface is dated from Wittenberg 24 Feb., 1522. The English version was made from the Latin by Miles Coverdale and was printed at the expense of William Marshall. Early in April, 1534, he wrote to Cromwell " As to the book of Constantine I have laid out all the money I can make and for lack of it cannot fetch the books from the printers. I will pay you before All Saints next and if I obtain the money, I shall be able to print the work De veteri et novo Deo immediately after Easter."

ORDINARY OF CHRISTIAN MEN.
4to. *Wynkyn de Worde. London,* 1506.

Title. Thordynary of | Crysten men | [Woodcut]. Leaf 217ᵇ *Colophon.* ⁋ Here endeth the boke named the ordynarye of | crysten men newely hystoryed and transla- | ted out of Frensshe in to Englysshe . En | prynted in the cyte of London in | the Fletestrete in the sygne | of yᵉ sonne by Wynkyn de worde . yᵉ yere | of our lorde. | M.cc | ccc | .vi. | ::

Collation. Aa⁴, A⁶, B–X, AA–MM⁴/⁸, NN⁴, OO, PP⁶; 218 leaves. 34 lines.

Leaf 1ᵃ Title, 1ᵇ–4ᵇ Table of contents, 5ᵃ–7ᵇ Prologue, 8ᵃ–217ᵇ Text, 218ᵃ W. de Worde's device 5, 218ᵇ Title-page repeated.   **[1273.]**

Wants leaves 1–4, 6–8, 10. With numerous woodcuts. This translation was made by Andrew Chertsey from L'Ordinaire des chrestiens, many editions of which were printed in France from about 1487 onwards.

PEROTTUS (NICOLAUS). Grammatica.
4to. *Nicholas de la Barre. Paris,* 1498.

Title. GRAMATICA | Nicolay Perotti cum arte metrica eiusdem nuper | emendata impressa cum summa orthographie et | diptongoᴚ obseruatiōe & ab aliis prorsus neglecta | ⁋ Item Guarinus Ueronensis de arte diptongā | di nuper castigatus | ⁋ Idem Regule decrescentis genitiuorum | [Device of N. de la Barre.] Leaf 132ᵃ *Colophon.* ⁋ Impressum parisius per | Nicolaū de barra in artib᾿ ma | gistrum cōmorantem in vico cy | thare ante scutū regis francie. | Die vero prima mensis : Iunii ; | Anno dñi M.CCCC.XCVIII.

Collation. A–C⁸, D⁶, E–G⁸, H⁶, I–L⁸, M, N⁶, O, P⁸, Q⁶, R⁸, S⁶; 132 leaves. 42 lines. With numbers to pages.

Leaf 1ᵃ Title, 1ᵇ–2ᵃ Address of Paulus Malleolus, 2ᵇ–132 Text, 132ᵇ Device. [*B.L.*]   **[1305⁷.]**

This edition appears to be entirely unknown.

POLITI (LANCELOTTO).   Excusatio disputationis contra Martinum [Lutherum]. 4to.   *Haeredes Philippi Iuntae. Florence,* 1521.

Leaf 1ᵃ begins: Fratris Ambrosii Chatharini ord. pred. Con | gregatiōis sancti Marci d' Florētia: Excu | satio disputationis contra Martinū | ad vniuersas ecclesias. | [*etc.*] Leaf 105ᵃ *Colophon.* Florentiæ per hæredes Philippi Iuntæ. | Anno Domini. M.D.XXI. | Die ultimo Aprilis.

Collation. a–m⁸, n¹⁰; 106 leaves. 29 lines. With headlines and numbers to pages.

Leaf 1ᵃ Title, etc., 1ᵇ Dedication to the Emperor Charles V, 2ᵃ–105ᵃ Text, 105ᵇ Errata, 106ᵃ blank, 106ᵇ [Junta device]. [*R.L.*]   [**1481²**.]

POMPONATIUS (PETRUS) [Pietro Pomponazzi].   De immortalitate animae.   12°. 1534 [1680].

Title [within border].   PETRI | POMPONATII | MANTVANII, | TRACTATVS | DE | IMMORTALITATE | ANIMÆ. | M.D.XXXIV.

Collation. A–F¹² [2]; 74 leaves. 31 lines. With headlines and numbers to pages.

Leaf 1ᵃ Title, 1ᵇ blank, 2 Proemium, 3ᵃ–74ᵃ Text, 74ᵇ blank. [*R.L.*]   [**302**.]

This is a reprint of the seventeenth century. A very full account of the book and its author will be found in the Essays and Papers of R. C. Christie, 1902, pp. 124–160.

PROCLUS, *Diadochus.*   Description of the world.
                              8°. *Robert Wyer. London.* [1550.]
Title. ℭ The Descripci- | on of the Sphere | or Frame of | the worlde. [Woodcut.] Leaf 24ᵇ *Colophon.* ℭ Imprynted by me Ro- | bert Wyer: Dwellynge at the | Sygne of S. Iohñ Euangelyst, | in S. Martyns Parysshe besyde | Charynge Crosse. | ℭ Cum priuilegio, Ad | imprimendum solum.

Collation. A–F⁴; 24 leaves. 23 lines. With headlines, but no numbers to pages.

Leaf 1ᵃ Title, 1ᵇ Table, 2ᵃ–4ᵃ Address to John Edwardes of Chyrcke, 4ᵇ–5ᵇ To the reader, 6ᵃ–24ᵇ Text. [*B.L.*]   [**46¹**.]

The woodcut on the title-page represents Ptolemy with a female figure.

The book was translated by William Salisbury the famous Welsh scholar.

Plomer, Robert Wyer No. 85.

QUATTUOR SERMONES.   fol.   *Richard Pynson.*   [*London*, 1493.]

Leaf 1ᵃ.   THE maister of sentence in the se | counde booke and the firste de | stinccion sayth. that the soue- | rayne cause why god made all creatu | res in heuyn erth or water was his ou | ne godenes by the whiche he wold that | some of theym sholde haue parte and | be communers of his euirlastinge blis [*etc.*].   Leaf 24, col. 2, line 19, vinculo delictorum : vt in resurrectio- | nis gloria inter sanctos et electos tuos | resuscitati respirent.   Per cristum do- | minum nostrum Amen. | Emprentyd by me Richarde Pinson. | [Pynson's device.]

Collation.   A–C⁸ ; 24 leaves.   40 lines.   No headlines or numbers to pages.

Leaf 1ᵃ–24ᵇ text. [*B.L.*]   [1944².]

At the end are two leaves of manuscript containing the "Form of Bydding of Bedys."

This book was printed as a supplement to Mirk's Liber Festivalis, and is usually bound with it.

RECORDE (ROBERT).   The castle of knowledge.
                              fol.   *Reginald Wolfe.   London*, 1556.
Title.   The Castle of Knowledge.   Leaf 152ᵃ *Colophon.*   Imprinted at London by Reginalde | Wolfe, Anno Domini, 1556.

Collation.   aᵃ, A–Z, &, ⁶ ; 152 leaves.   35 lines.   With headlines and numbers to pages.

Leaf 1ᵃ Title, 1ᵇ Contents, 2 Dedication to Q. Mary, 3 Dedication to Cardinal Pole, 4ᵃ–7ᵇ Preface, 8ᵃ Admonition, 8ᵇ Woodcut, 9ᵃ–150ᵇ Text, 151ᵃ Index of chapters, 152ᵃ Errata, 152ᵇ blank. [*R.L.*]   [2049¹.]

The title-page is filled with an elaborate allegorical woodcut of the Castle of Knowledge with Knowledge standing on a cube holding a pair of compasses on one side, and Ignorance standing on a globe with a wheel of fortune on the other.

REYNARD THE FOX.   fol.   [*William Caxton.   Westminster*, 1489.]

Leaf 1ᵃ [Caxton's device].   ⫿ This is the table of the historye of Reynart the foxe.   Leaf 3ᵃ.   ⫿ How the lyon kynge of alle bestys sent out hys maūde | mentys that alle beestys sholde come to hys feest and court, | ⫿ Capitulo Primo | IT was aboute yᵉ tyme of penthecoste or whytsontyde | that the wodes comynly be lusty and gladsom, And | trees clad with leuis & blossoms and yᵉ ground wyth | herbes & floures [*etc.*]   Leaf 70ᵇ, line 30. rewle vs to his playsir. And her wyth wil I leue ffor w | hat haue I to wryte of thyse mys dedis I haue yuowh [*sic*] to doo | [all after wanting].

Collation. [2] a–h⁸, i⁶ ; 72 leaves. 31–2 lines. No headlines or numbers to pages.

Leaf 1ᵃ Device, etc., 1ᵇ–2ᵇ Table, Preface, 3ᵃ–end Text. [*B.L.*] [**1796.**]
The only copy known of this edition. Imperfect at end.

ROTE OR MIRROR OF CONSOLATION.
4to. *Wynkyn de Worde. Westminster* [1499.]
Title. ℂ The Rote or myrour of consolacyon & conforte. | [Woodcut.]
Leaf 2ᵃ. ℂ The Rote or myrour of consolacyon & cōforte. | PEr multas tribulaciones oportet | introire in regnum dei [*etc.*] Leaf 64ᵃ, line 9. ℂ Here endeth the Rote or myrour of | consolacyon and conforte. Em- | prynted at Westmyster by Wyn- | ken de Worde. | [W. de Worde's device 3.]

Collation. A–E⁸, F–I⁶ ; 64 leaves. 29 lines. No headlines or numbers to pages.

Leaf 1ᵃ Title, 1ᵇ [Woodcut], 2ᵃ–64ᵃ Text, 64ᵇ Woodcut. [*B.L.*] [**1254⁴.**]

On the title-page is a woodcut of the service of mass, with seven persons before the altar ; two angels above it hold a monstrance. On the reverse of the title-page and last page is the cut of the Crucifixion. Between the printing of the first sheet and the last this woodcut had been cracked. From this fact and the state of the device the book can be ascribed to the second half of 1499. This is the only copy known of this edition : the unique copy of an edition printed about 1496 is in the library of Durham Cathedral.

Early autograph on title " Nico. Atkinson."

THE ROYAL BOOK. 4to. *Richard Pynson. London,* 1507.
Title. The boke na- | med the royall. Leaf 5ᵃ. ℂ Here after ben conteyned and declared the | x. cōmaundementes of the lawe whiche | our lorde delyuered vnto Moyses the pro | phete for to preche to the people for to hol | de and kepe. Capitulo. primo. | [*etc.*]. Leaf 186ᵃ. . . . whyche | translacyon or reducynge out of frensshe in to englysshe | was achyued, fynysshed & accomplysshed the .xiii. day | of Septembre in yᵉ yere of thyncarnacyon of our lorde. | M.CCCCC. &. vii. The .xxii. yere of the reygne of kyn- | ge Henry the seuenth. | ℂ Here endeth the boke called

the ryoall. [*sic*] Enprynted at | London in fletestrete at the sygne of saynt George by | Rycharde Pynson.

Collation. [4] A–Z, Aa–Ff⁶, Gg, Hh⁴ ; 186 leaves. 32 lines. No headlines or numbers to pages.

Leaf 1ᵃ Title, 1ᵇ–4ᵃ Table, 4ᵇ Woodcut, 5ᵃ–185ᵇ Text, 185ᵇ–186ᵃ Epilogue and colophon, 186ᵇ Pynson's device. [*B.L.*] [1011¹.]

The epilogue has been copied exactly from Caxton's edition with the one alteration of the date and regnal year. The day of the month has been left as in Caxton's epilogue, an unfortunate blunder, for in this edition it reads "xiii day of Septembre . . . M.CCCCCVII. the XXII yere of . . . Henry the seuenth." But 13 Sept. 22 Henry VII was in 1506. It has been asserted that the Pynson and W. de Worde editions of 1507 are identical except for the necessary change of name in the colophon. I have not been able to compare the two side by side, but both certainly have the misprint "ryoall" in the colophon. If it is the case, such errors would point to De Worde having been the printer rather than Pynson.

THE RUTTER OF THE SEA.

8°. *William Copland. London* [1555.]

Title [within borders]. ℂ The Rut | ter of the Sea, wᵗ the hauõs, | rodes, soundinges, kennyn- | ges, wyndes, floudes and | ebbs, daungers and costes | of dyuers regions wyth the | lawes of the yle of Au- | leron and the iudge | mentes of the- | Sea. ℂ with a Rutter of the | Northe added to | the same. Leaf 44ᵃ *Colophon.* Imprinted at London | by wyllyam Cop- | land.

Collation. A–E⁸, F⁴ ; 44 leaves. 24 lines. No headlines or numbers to pages.

Leaf 1ᵃ Title, 1ᵇ blank, 2ᵃ–4ᵃ Prologue of Robert Copland, 4ᵇ–39ᵃ Text, 39ᵇ–44ᵃ New Rutter by Richard Proude, 1541. [*B.L.*] [96¹.]

Translated by Robert Copland from Le grand Routier de la Mer by Pierre Garcia.

SAINT GERMAIN (CHRISTOPHER). The division between the spiritualty and temporalty. 8°. *Thomas Berthelet. London* [1530.]

Title [within border]. ⟴ A Treatise concer- | nynge the diuisi- | on betwene | the spi- | ritu- | altie and tem- | poraltie. | ⟴ Leaf 47ᵃ *Colophon.* ⟴ Londini in edibus Thome Ber- | theleti, prope aquagium sitis | sub intersignio Lucre | cie Romane | excus. | CVM PRIVILEGIO.

Collation. A–F⁸ ; 48 leaves. 27 lines. With headlines and numbers to pages.

Leaf 1ᵃ Title, 1ᵇ Introduction, 2ᵃ–45ᵃ Text, 45ᵇ–47ᵃ Table, 47ᵇ, 48 blank. [*B.L.*]   [**368**¹.]

This book called forth an attack from Sir Thomas More entitled an Apology, which was answered by " Salem and Bizance."

SAINT GERMAIN (CHRISTOPHER). Salem and Bizance.
                    8°.   *Thomas Berthelet. London,* 1533.
Title. SALEM | AND | BI- | ZANCE. Leaf 2ᵃ. ℂ A dialogue betwixte two englyshe | men, wherof one was called Sa- | lem, and the other Bizance.   Leaf 107ᵃ *Colophon.*   LONDINI IN AEDIBVS | THOMAE BERTHELETI. | M.D.XXXIII. | CVM PRIVILEGIO.

Collation.   A–N⁸, O⁴ ; 108 leaves.   24 lines.   With headlines and numbers to pages.

Leaf 1ᵃ Title, 1ᵇ blank, 2ᵃ–3ᵃ Introduction, 3ᵇ–106ᵇ Text, 107ᵃ Errata and *colophon,* 107ᵇ, 108 blank. [*B.L.*]   [**752**¹.]

SAVONAROLA (GIROLAMO).   Exposition upon the 30ᵗʰ Psalm.
        4to. [*John Byddell for William Marshall.*] [*London.*] [1535.]
Begins Leaf 1ᵃ. ℂ A goodly exposition vpon the . xxx . psalme | In te domine speraui. | [*etc.*]   Leaf 14ᵃ ends. ℂ An ende of the exposition of Hierome of Ferrarie | vpon the psalme of In te domine speraui, | whiche preuented by deathe he | coulde not fynyshe.

Collation.   a–c⁴, d² ; 14 leaves.   32 lines.   With headlines ; no numbers to pages.

Leaf 1ᵃ–14ᵃ Text, 14ᵇ Marshall's arms.   [**1374**².]

Printed as a supplement to the Horae ad usum Sarum of 1535.

SKELTON (JOHN).   Epitaph of Jasper, Duke of Bedford.
              4to. *Richard Pynson.* [*London.*] [1496.]
Title [woodcut].   The Epitaffe of the moste noble & valyaunt | Iasper late duke of Beddeforde.   Leaf 9ᵇ line 1.   Kynges prynces moste souerayne of renoune, | Remembre oure maister that gone is byfore. | This worlde is casual, nowe vp, nowe downe. | Wherfore do for your silfe I can say no more. | Amen | Honor tibi deus, gloria, et laus. | Qd' Smerte maister, de ses ouzeaus.

Collation. A⁶, B⁴; 10 leaves. 29 lines. Without headlines or numbers to pages.

Leaf 1ᵃ Title, 1ᵇ blank, 2ᵃ–9ᵇ Text, 10ᵃ blank, 10ᵇ Pynson's device. [*B.L.*] [**1254⁵.**]

The only copy known.

STANBRIDGE (JOHN). Accidence.

4to. *Richard Pynson.* [*London.*] [1496.]

Leaf 1ᵃ. WHat shalt thou doo whanne thou | haste an englissh to make in laten | I shal reherce myn englissh ones | twyes or thries and loke oute my | principal verbe *&* aske this questy | on [*etc.*]. Leaf 11ᵇ, line 17. Nemo caret quinto pariter numeroɋ secundo | Sic finitur hoc opusculum | ⊄ Emprented by Richard Pynson : Leaf 12ᵃ blank. Leaf 12ᵇ Pynson's device 2.

Collation. ab⁶; 12 leaves. 29 lines. No headlines or numbers to pages. [*B.L.*] [**1305⁴.**]

It is clear from the condition of the printer's device that the book must have been printed in 1496–7. The only copy known.

STATUTES. Edward III–Henry VIII.

fol. *William Middleton.* *London* [1545.]

⊄ The great boke of statutes cō- | teynyng all the statutes made in the parlyamentes from the | begynnynge of the fyrst yere of the raigne of kynge Edwarde the thyrde tyll | the begynnyng of the . xxxiiii . yere of the most gracyous raigne of our soueraigne lorde kyng Henry the . VIII. | [Woodcut.] ⚜ : Cum privilegio . . . Leaf 338ᵇ *Colophon.* ⚜ : Imprynted at London by | UUyllyam Meddelton Cum priui- | legio Regali.

Collation. *, A⁶, B, C⁴, +², A–M⁶, N⁴, O–V⁶, X, Y⁴, A–Y⁶, A–I⁶, K⁴, A–L⁶; 404 leaves. 45 lines. With headlines; no numbers to pages.

Leaf 1ᵃ Title, 1ᵇ Woodcut of royal arms, 2ᵃ–22ᵇ Tables, 23ᵃ–148ᵇ Edward III and Richard II, 149ᵃ–280ᵃ Henry IV, V, VI, 280ᵇ blank, 281ᵃ–338ᵇ Edward IV, Richard III, 339ᵃ–404ᵃ Henry VII, 404ᵇ blank.

[**1992¹.**]

The index and statutes in this volume only go to the end of the reign of Henry VII.

STATUTES.   19. Henry VII.   fol. *Richard Pynson.   London* [1505.]

Title. Anno Decimonono Henrici septimi. | Statuta in parliamēto apud westmonasteriü vicesimo quī | to die Ianuarii. Anno regni metuedissimi Regis Anglie & Frā | cie : ac domini hibernie Henrici septimi decimonono tento ꝑ bo | no publico subditorū suorum inter cetera edita. [Woodcut.] Leaf 18^b *Colophon.* ⬫ Emprented at London in Flete strete at the | signe of the George by saint Dustones | chyrche By me Rycharde Pyn- | son Squyer and prenter | vnto the Kynges | noble grace. | [Pynson's device 3].

Collation. 1^6, m^8, n^4 ; 18 leaves.   42 lines.   With headlines.

Leaf 1^a Title, 1^b Table, 2^a–18^b Text.   [1992².]

On the title-page is a large woodcut of the king on his throne surrounded by six councillors.

—— Henry VIII.   fol. *Thomas Berthelet. London,* 1543 [–1547.]

Title. ⬫ THE Second Volume | conteyninge those Statutes, | VVhiche haue ben made in | the tyme of the most vi- | ctorious reigne of our | most gracious soue- | raigne lorde kyng | Henry the | Eyght. | ⬫ | ⬫ LONDINI in ædibus Thomæ Bertheleti | Typographi regii excus. | ANNO verbi incarnati .MD.XLIII. | CVM priuilegio ad imprimen- | dum solum.

Collation. A^6 ; 6 leaves.   59 lines.   With headlines ; no numbers to pages.

Leaf 1^a Title, 1^b blank, 2^a–6^b Index.   [1993.]

Each year in the following collection has been printed separately and then collected and issued with a general title, some are original issues, others are reprints of a few years later. The addition of the words "ad imprimendum solum" in any colophon shows that the printing must be later than 1538.

—— 1.

Title. ⬫ ANNO PRIMO | HENRICI OCTAVI. | [*etc.*].   Leaf 10^b *Colophon.* Thomas Berthelet regius impressor | excudebat. Cum privilegio.

Collation. A^6, B^4 ; 10 leaves.   43 lines.   With headlines and numbers to pages.

Leaf 1^a Title, 1^b Table, 2^a–10^b Statutes.

STATUTES. 2.

Title. ꙮ ANNO TERTIO | HENRICI OCTAVI. | [*etc.*]. Leaf 53[b]
Colophon. Tho. Bertheleti regius impressor excudebat. Cum priuilegio
ad imprimendum solum.

Collation. A–I[6] ; 54 leaves. 43 lines. With headlines and numbers
to pages.

Leaf 1[a] Title, 1[b] Table, 2[a]–14[a] Statutes An. 3, 14[b] blank, 15[a] Title,
15[b] Table, 16[a]–22[b] Statutes An. 4, 23[a] Title, 23[b] Table, 24[a]–28[b] Statutes
An. 5, 29[a] Title, 29[b] Table, 30[a]–45[b] Statutes An. 6, 46[a] Title, 46[b] Table,
47[a]–53[b] Statutes An. 7, 54 blank.

—— 3.

Title. ꙮ ANNO XIIII ET | XV HENRICI OCTAVI. | [*etc.*].
Leaf 15[b] *Colophon.* Thomas Berthelet regius impressor | excudebat.
Cum priuilegio.

Collation. AB[6], C[4] ; 16 leaves. 43 lines. With headlines and
numbers to pages.

Leaf 1[a] Title, 1[b] Table, 2[a]–15[b] Statutes, 16 blank.

—— 4.

Title [within border]. ANNO. XXI. | HENRICI | VIII. | [*etc.*].
Leaf 27[b] *Colophon.* LONDINI IN AEDIBVS THOMAE BER- |
THELETI REGII IMPRES- | SORIS. | CVM PRIVILEGIO.

Collation. AD[6], E[4] ; 28 leaves. 44 lines. With headlines and numbers
to pages.

Leaf 1[a] Title, 1[b] Table, 2[a]–27[b] Statutes, 28 blank.

—— 5.

Title. ANNO VICECIMO SE- | CVNDO HENRICI | OCTAVI. |
[*etc.*]. Leaf 24[a] *Colophon.* Tho. Berthelet regius impressor excudebat. |
CVM PRIVILEGIO.

Collation. A–D[6] ; 24 leaves. 43 lines. With headlines and numbers
to pages.

Leaf 1[a] Title, 1[b] Table, 2[a]–24[a] Statutes, 24[b] blank.

STATUTES. 6.

Title. ☙ ANNO. XXIII. HENRICI | OCTAVI. | [*etc.*].   Leaf 28ª
Colophon.   ⓠ Imprynted at London in Fletestrete by | Thomas Berthelet
prynter to | the kynges most noble | grace.   Cum pri- | uilegio.
Collation.   A–D⁶, E⁴ ; 28 leaves.   43 lines.   With headlines ; no
numbers to pages.
Leaf 1ª Title, 1ᵇ Table, 2ª–28ª Statutes, 28ᵇ blank.

——— 7.

Title. ANNO XXIIII | HENRICI | VIII. | . . . LONDINI in ædibus
Thomæ Ber- | theleti typis impress. | Cum priuilegio ad imprimen- | dum
solum. | ANNO. M.D. XLVI.
Collation.   A–C⁶ ; 18 leaves.   44 lines.   With headlines and numbers
to pages.
Leaf 1ª Title, 1ᵇ Table, 2ª–18ᵇ Statutes.

——— 8.

Title. ☙ ANNO. XXV. | HENRICI | VIII. | . . . ☙ LONDINI ☙ |
IN OFFICINA THOMAE BAR- | THELETI TYPIS | IMPRES. |
CVM PRIVILEGIO AD IMPRI- | MENDVM SOLVM.
Collation.   A–G⁶ ; 42 leaves.   44 lines.   With headlines ; no numbers
to pages.
Leaf 1ª Title, 1ᵇ Table, 2ª–41ᵇ Statutes, 42 blank.

——— 9.

Title. ANNO. XXVI. HENRICI | OCTAVI. | [*etc.*].   Leaf 26ᵇ
Colophon. ☙ THOMAS BERTHELETUS RE- | GIVS IMPRESSOR
EX- | CVDEBAT. | ☙ Cum priuilegio ad imprimendum solum.
Collation.   A–C⁶, D⁸ ; 26 leaves.   44 lines.   With headlines ; no
numbers to pages.
Leaf 1ª Title, 1ᵇ Table, 2ª–26ᵇ Statutes.

——— 10.

Title [within border].   ANNO XXVII. | HENRICI | VIII. | . . .
THOMAS BERTHELET | typographus regius excudebat. | ANNO.
M.D. XLVI. | Cum priuilegio ad impri- | mendum solum.
Collation.   A–G⁶, H⁴ ; 46 leaves.   44 lines.   With headlines and
numbers to pages.
Leaf 1ª Title, 1ᵇ Table, 2ª–46ᵇ Statutes.

STATUTES. 11.

Title [within border]. ANNO. XXVIII. | HENRICI | VIII. | . . .
THO. BERTHELET RE- | GIS IMPRESSOR EX- | CVDEBAT, |
CVM PRIVILEGIO.

Collation. A–C⁶, D⁸ ; 26 leaves. 44 lines. With headlines ; no numbers
to pages.

Leaf 1ᵃ Title, 1ᵇ Table, 2ᵃ–26ᵇ Statutes.

—— 12.

Title. ✿ ANNO TRICESIMO PRIMO | HENRICI OCTAVI. | . . .
✿ LONDINI. | ✿ ANNO VERBI IN- | CARNATI | M.D.XXXIX.
Leaf 29ᵇ *Colophon.* Londini in ædibus Thomæ Berthe- | leti typis impress. |
Cum priuilegio Ad imprimen- | dum solum. | ANNO. M.D.XXXIX.

Collation. A–E⁶ ; 30 leaves. 44 lines. With headlines and numbers
to pages.

Leaf 1ᵃ Title, 1ᵇ Table, 2ᵃ–29ᵇ Statutes, 30 blank.

—— 13.

Title. ✿ ANNO XXXII. | HENRICI OCTAVI. | . . . ANNO.
M.D.XL. Leaf 72ᵇ *Colophon.* LONDINI ex ædibus Thomæ Bertheleti |
CVM priuilegio ad impri- | mendum solum.

Collation. A–M⁶ ; 72 leaves. 44 lines. With headlines and numbers
to pages.

Leaf 1ᵃ Title, 1ᵇ Table, 2ᵃ–72ᵇ Statutes.

—— 14.

Title [within border]. ANNO TRICESIMO | TERTIO HENRICI |
OCTAVI. | [*etc.*]. Leaf 70ᵃ *Colophon.* LONDINI ex officina Thomæ
Ber- | theleti typis impress. | Cum priuilegio ad imprimendum | solum. |
✿ ANNO. M.D.XLII.

Collation. A–L⁶, M⁴ ; 70 leaves. 44 lines. With headlines, partly
paged.

Leaf 1ᵃ Title, 1ᵇ Table, 2ᵃ–70ᵃ Statutes, 70ᵇ blank.

—— 15.

Title. ✿ ANNO TRICESIMO QVAR- | TO ET QVINTO HENRI- |
CI OCTAVI. | . . . IMPRINTED at London in Fletestrete by Thomas |
Barthelet printer to the kynges hyghnes, the | firste day of Iune, the yere

of our | Lorde. M.DXLIII. | CVM priuilegio ad imprimendum solum. Leaf 66ᵃ *Colophon.* IMPRINTED at London in Fletestrete by Thomas | Berthelet printer to the kynges highnes, the .iii. | daie of Ianuarie, the yere of our Lorde. | M.D.XLVII. | CVM priuilegio ad imprimendum solum.

Collation. A–E⁶, F⁴, G–K⁶, L⁸ ; 66 leaves. 44 lines. With headlines ; no numbers to pages.

Leaf 1ᵃ Title, 1ᵇ Table, 2ᵃ–34ᵃ Statutes, 34ᵇ blank, 35ᵃ–52ᵃ Statutes, 52ᵇ blank, 53ᵃ–66ᵃ Statutes, 66ᵇ blank.

STATUTES. 16.

Title. ✿ HENRY THE | EYGHT BY THE GRACE OF | GOD [*etc.*] [xxxv] . . . ✿ LONDINI ✿ | IN ædibus Thomæ Bertheleti regii im- | pressoris typis excusum. | ANNO uerbi incarnati .M.D.XLIIII. | CVM PRIVILEGIO AD IMPRI- | MENDVM SOLVM. Leaf 31ᵇ *Colophon.* IMPRINTED at London in Fletestrete by Thomas Bar- | thelet prynter to the kynges hyghnes, the .ix. | daye of Apryll, the yere of oure Lorde. | M.D.XLIIII. | CVM PRIVILEGIO AD IMPRIMEN- | DVM SOLVM.

Collation. A–D⁶, E⁴, F⁴ ; 32 leaves. 44 lines. With headlines ; no numbers to pages.

Leaf 1ᵃ Title, 1ᵇ Table, 2ᵃ–28ᵃ Statutes, 28ᵇ blank, 29ᵃ–31ᵇ Act concerning pardon, 32 blank.

—— 17.

Title [within border]. Statutes made in the | parliament, holden at westminster | in the . XXXVII . | yere of the reygne of | the moste renoumed HENRY | the eyght, [*etc.*]. . . THOMAS BERTHELET | typographus regius excudebat. | ANNO, M.D.XLVI. | Cum priuilegio ad imprimen- | dum solum. Leaf 36ᵇ *Colophon.* LONDINI in ædibus Thomæ Ber- | theleti typis impress. | Cum priuilegio ad imprimen- | dum solum. | ANNO . M.D.XLVI.

Collation. A–F⁶ ; 36 leaves. 44 lines. With headlines ; no numbers to pages.

Leaf 1ᵃ Title, 1ᵇ Table, 2ᵃ–36ᵇ Text.

STATUTES. 18.

Leaf 1 begins : Anno tricesimo septimo Henrici octaui. | ℭ The acte concernyng the Subsidie | graunted of the Temporaltie. | [*etc.*] Leaf 16^b *Colophon.* LONDINI in ædibus Thomæ Bertheleti typis impress. | Cum priuilegio ad imprimen- | dum solum. | ANNO. M.D.XLVI.

Collation. A, B⁶, C⁴ ; 16 leaves. 44 lines. With headlines ; no numbers to pages.

Leaf 1ª–16^b Text.

―― Edward VI–12 Elizabeth.
fol. *R. Grafton and J. Cawood. London,* 1548, etc.
Title [within border]. ⮜ A table | to al the Statutes made from | the beginning of the raigne of | Kyng Edwarde the VI. vnto this | present . xii. yeare of the reigne | of oure moste gratious | and soueraigne Ladye | Queene Elizabeth. | (. ˙.) | In ædibus Richardi | Totelli. | Cum priuilegio.

Collation. A⁶ ; 6 leaves. 54 lines. With headlines ; no numbers to pages.

Leaf 1ª Title, 1^b blank, 2ª–6^b Index. [1994.]

―― 1.

Title [within border]. ℭ Anno primo Edwar- | DI SEXTI. | ℭ Statutes | [*etc.*]. *Colophon* leaf 38^b. ℭ Excusum Londini, in Ædibus Richardi Graftoni, | Regii Impressoris. | Anno M.D.xlviij. | ℭ Cum Priuilegio ad imprimendum.

Collation. A–E⁶, F⁸ ; 38 leaves. 44 lines. With headlines and numbers to pages.

Leaf 1ª Title, 1^b Index, 2ª–38^b Text.

―― 2.

Title [within border]. ANNO SECUNDO | ET TERTIO EDVARDI| SEXTI. | ⮜ ACTES | [*etc.*]. Leaf 68^b *Colophon.* RICHARDVS GRAF | tonus, Typographus Regius excudebat. | Anno Domini . 1552. | Cum Priuilegio ad Imprimen- | dum solum.

Collation. A–G⁶, H⁴, I–K⁶, L⁴, M⁶ ; 68 leaves. 44 lines. With headlines and numbers to pages.

Leaf 1ª Title, 1^b Table, 2ª–68^b Text.

STATUTES.   3.

Title [within border].   ℭ ANNO III ET IIII. | EDVVARDI SEXTI. | ❧ Actes made | [*etc.*].   Leaf 32ᵇ *Colophon*.   ℭ Imprinted at London by Richard Grafton | Printer to the Kinges Maiestie. | 1553. | Cum priuilegio.

Collation.   A–D⁶, E, F⁴, ; 32 leaves.   45 lines.   With headlines and numbers to pages.

Leaf 1ᵃ Title, 1ᵇ Table, 2ᵃ–28ᵃ Text, 28ᵇ blank, 29ᵃ–32ᵇ Act of pardon.

—— 4.

Title [within border].   ℭ ANNO QVINTO ET | SEXTO | EDVVARDI | SEXTI. | ❧ Actes made | [*etc.*].   Leaf 33ᵇ *Colophon*. ℭ RICHARDVS GRAFTONVS. | Tipographus Regius excudebat. | Mense Iun. | 1552. | ℭ Cum priuilegio ad imprimendum solum.

Collation.   A–E⁶, F⁴; 34 leaves.   45 lines.   With headlines and numbers to pages.

Leaf 1ᵃ Title, 1ᵇ Table, 2ᵃ–33ᵇ Text, 34 blank.

—— 5.

Title [within border].   ANNO SEPTIMO | EDVVARDI SEXTI. | ❧ ACTES ❧ | [*etc.*].   Leaf 44ᵃ *Colophon*.   Londini in ædibus Richardi Graftoni | typographi Regii excusum. | Mense Aprilis. | Anno Domini . M.D.LIII. | Cum priuilegio ad imprimendnm solum.

Collation.   A–F⁶, G, H⁴; 44 leaves.   44 lines.   With headlines and numbers to pages.

Leaf 1ᵃ Title, 1ᵇ Table, 2ᵃ–44ᵃ Text, 44ᵇ blank.

—— 6.

Title [within border].   Anno Mariæ Primo. | ¶ Actes [*etc.*].   Leaf 18ᵃ *Colophon*.   Excusum Londini in edibus Iohannis Cawo- | di, Typographi Regiæ Ma- | iestatis. | Anno M.D.Liiii. | Mense Maio. | Cum priuilegio Reginæ Mariæ.

Collation.   A, B⁶, C⁴. D²; 18 leaves.   44 lines.   With headlines ; no numbers to pages.

Leaf 1ᵃ Title, 1ᵇ Table, 2ᵃ–18ᵃ Text, 18ᵇ blank.

G

STATUTES. 7.

Title [within border]. ANNO MARIA | PRIMO. | ¶ Actes [*etc.*]. Leaf 27ᵇ *Colophon.* EXCVSVM LONDINI IN ÆDIBVS | Iohannis Cawoodi, Typographi Regiæ | Maiestatis . | Anno Domini . M.D.LIIII. | Cum priuilegio ad imprimendum solum.

Collation. A–D⁶, E⁴; 28 leaves.   44 lines.   With headlines and numbers to pages.

Leaf 1ᵃ Title, 1ᵇ Table, 2ᵃ Act repealing treasons, 3 blank, 4ᵃ Title, 4ᵇ Table, 5ᵃ–27ᵇ Text, 28 blank.

—— 8.

Title [within border].   Anno secundo & tertio Phi· | lippi & Mariæ. | Actes [*etc.*].   Leaf 58ᵇ *Colophon.*   Excusum Londini in ædibus Iohannis Cawodi | Tipographi Regiæ Maiestatis. | Anno Domini . 1555. | Cum priuilegio Regiæ Maiestatis.

Collation. A–I⁶, K⁴; 58 leaves.   44 lines.   With headlines; no numbers to pages.

Leaf 1ᵃ Title, 1ᵇ Table, 2ᵃ–58ᵇ Text.

[Remaining acts after 1557.]

SULPITIUS (IOANNES) Verulanus.   Opus grammatices.

4to.   *Richard Pynson.   London,* 1498.

Leaf 1ᵃ.   Sulpitii Uerulani oratoris prestantissi | mi opus grammatices insigne feliciter | incipit | [Woodcut].   Leaf 52ᵇ, line 35 *Colophon.* ℂ| Sulpitiano grammatices opusculo vigilanter | punctuato & correcto iamiam extra barrã noui | templi londoniarũ p Richardũ Pynson impres- | so finis imponitur : Anno salutis M . cccc . xcviii.   Leaf 62ᵃ line 21. excitasse librum hoc carmine finiam. | Finis.

Collation. a–c,⁸ d–g⁶, h⁸, i⁶; 62 leaves.   42 lines.   With headlines and numbers to pages.

Leaf 1ᵃ Title, 1ᵇ blank, 2ᵃ De arte punctuandi, 2ᵇ Verses, 3ᵃ–62ᵃ Text, 62ᵇ Device 2.   [*B.L.*]   [1305⁶.]

On the title-page is a woodcut of a master and his pupils.

The only other copy known is in the British Museum.

TINDALE (WILLIAM).   The obedience of a Christian man.
8°.   Hans Luft.   Marlborow [Antwerp], 1528.

Title [within borders].   The obediē | ce of a Christen man and how Chr | istē rulers ought to gouerne, | where in also (yf thou ma- | rke diligently) th- | ou shalt fynde | eyes to pe- | rceaue | the | crafty conveyaūce of all | iugglers.   Leaf 168ᵇ *Colophon.*   ⊄ At Marlborow in the lāde of | Hesse The seconde daye of Octo | ber . Anno . M.CCCCC.xxviij, by | me Hans luft.

Collation.   a–xˢ ; 168 leaves.   31-32 lines.   Without headlines ; with numbers to pages.

Leaf 1ᵃ Title, 1ᵇ blank, 2ᵃ–20ᵇ W. Tindale to the reader, 21ᵃ–24ᵇ Prologue, 25ᵃ–161ᵃ Text, 161ᵃ–168ᵃ Table, 168ᵃ–168ᵇ Errata.   [*B.L.*]   [**235.**]

—— The obedience of a christian man.
4to.   [*William Hill.*]   [*London.*] [1548.]

Title [within border].   ⊄ THE | Obedyence of | A Christian man : And how christen | Rulers ought to gouerne : wher- | in also (yf thou marke dyly- | gentlye) thou shalte finde | eyes to perceyue the | craftye conueigh- | aunce of all | Jugglers.   Reade (whensoeuer thou | Readeste good Christen | Reader) with a pure af- | fection, and vprighte | Judgementes to Godes | moste holy Booke. · . | : : 🙶❀🙷   Leaf 138ᵇ ends.   ypocrytes loue sacryfyce and offerynges Cii. | ⊄ Finis.

Collation.   A⁴, B–Rˢ, S⁶ ; 138 leaves.   32 lines.   With headlines and numbers to pages.

Leaf 1ᵃ Title, 1ᵇ blank, 2ᵃ–17ᵃ W. Tindale to the reader, 17ᵇ–20ᵇ Prologue, 21ᵃ–133ᵃ Text, 133ᵇ–138ᵇ Index.   [*B.L.*]   [**1028¹.**]

—— The parable of the wicked mammon.
4to.   *William Hill.   London* [1548.]

Title [within borders].   ⊄ The parable | Of the wycked mammon | taken out of the . xvi. Ca. | of Luke with an expo | sicyon thervpon la- | tely corrected & | prynted. | (.) | Luce . xvi | Facite vobis amicos de | mammon iniquitatis | 🙶❀🙷   Leaf 60ᵃ *Colophon.*   ⊄ Imprynted at London at the sygne | of the hill by Wyllyam hill | The xv day of september.

Collation.   A, B⁴, C–Gˢ, H⁴, Iˢ ; 60 leaves.   32 lines.   With headlines and numbers to pages.

Leaf 1ᵃ Title, 1ᵇ To the reader, 2ᵃ–4ᵇ W. Tindale to the reader, 5ᵃ–56ᵇ Text, 57ᵃ–60ᵃ Notes of the book, 60ᵇ blank.   [*B.L.*]   [**1028².**]

H

TORNIELLO (FRANCISCO).   Opera del modo de fare le littere majuscole
    antique.   4to.   *Gotardo da Ponte.   Milan*, 1517.

Title. ❡ Opera del modo de fare le littere maiuscole antique, conmesura |
de circino : *&* resone de penna, composita per Francisco | Torniello da
Novaria scriptore professo. | [Woodcut.]   Leaf 26ᵇ *Colophon.*   Nel anno
de lo aduento del signore : | Mille : con cinquecento : e decesepte. |
Gotardo . qual de libri e stampatore : | Dicto da ponte : de augustora di
septe. | Ha finito questa opera : ad honore | De quelli : che in uirtute se
dilecte. | Acio dei modi certificati : | Che in scriuer uoleno essere seruati.

Collation.   [a, bˢ, c¹⁰] ; 26 leaves.   32 lines.   No headlines or numbers
to pages.

Leaf 1ᵃ Title, 1ᵇ Preface, 2ᵃ–26ᵇ Text. [*R.L.*]   [**1512¹.**]

This work is on the mathematically designing of letters, and contains a
number of large diagrams.

TREATISE OF LOVE.
                        fol.   *Wynkyn de Worde.*   [*Westminster*] [1493].

Leaf 1ᵃ.   ❡ This tretyse is of love and spe | kyth of iiij of the most
specyall lo | uys that ben in the worlde and she | wyth veryly and perfitely
bi gret | [*etc.*].   Leaf 48ᵃ ends : Whiche boke was lately transla- | ted
oute of frensh in to englisshe | by a Right well dysposed persone, | for by
cause the sayd persone thoug | hte it necessary to al deuoute peple to
rede | or to here it redde, And also | caused the sayd boke to be enpryn- |
ted. | [Wynkyn de Worde's device 1].

Collation.   A–Hˢ ; 48 leaves.   36 lines.   No headlines or numbers to
pages. [*B.L.*]   [**2051².**]

This copy wants two leaves in signature B.

This book could not have been printed before 1493, as it is stated in the
prologue that the translation was made in that year.

TURNER (WILLIAM).   The hunting of the Romish wolf.
                        8°. [*Christopher Froschover.*] [*Zurich.*] [1554.]

Title.   The Huntyng of the | Romyshe Vuolfe, ma | de by Vuylliam
Tur- | ner doctour of | PHISIK. | ❡ Take hede of false Prophetes,
whyche | come vnto you in Shepes clothyng, | but wythin, are rauenyng |
Wolues. | +   Ends leaf 43ᵃ : fare ye well . Foster . God graunt | that we
maye mete mery to- | gether after the ende of | the parliament, | Hunter. |
Amen. | ☞

Collation. A–E⁸, F⁴ ; 44 leaves. 30 lines. No headlines or numbers to pages.

Leaf 1ᵃ Title, 1ᵇ–3ᵃ Introductory letter, 3ᵇ The Romish Fox speaketh, 4ᵃ–43ᵃ Text, 43ᵇ, 44 blank. [*B.L.*]   [209 ⁷.]

Wants last leaf.

VERINI (GIOVAMBAPTISTA). Luminario. De elementis litterarum.
                                                4to. [*Florence.*] [1526.]

Title [within border]. INCIPIT | LIBER PRI | MVS ELEMENTO | rum Litterarum Ioan | nis Baptiste de Ve | rinis Florentini | nouiter im | pressus. | [Six lines of verse.] CON GRATIA | ET PRIVILEGIO | PER ANNI. X. Leaf 63ᵇ *Colophon.* Hoc opus infectum videris si sordibus vllis : | Parce iuuentuti : temporibusq͒ simul. | Puchrius edetur studio maiore : vel arte : | Ipso Dante : breui : cunctipotente Deo.

Collation. A–N, [O–Q]⁴ ; 64 leaves. 30 lines. With headlines and numbers to pages.

Leaf 1ᵃ Title, 1ᵇ Verses to the reader, 2ᵃ Proemium, 2ᵇ–16ᵇ Book I, 17ᵃ Title, 17ᵇ–32ᵇ Book II, 33ᵃ Title, 33ᵇ–49ᵇ Book III, 50ᵃ Title, 50ᵇ–64ᵃ Book IV, 64ᵇ blank. [*R.L.*]   [1512².]

This very rare work on handwriting contains models of all the various hands. From the text we learn that the author was a bookseller of Florence, and that it was compiled in 1526. Though the title is in Latin, the rest of the book is in Italian.

VINCENTIUS. The mirror of the world.
                            fol. *William Caxton.* [*Westminster.*] [1490.]

Leaf 1 begins : HEre begynneth yᵉ table of the rubrices of this presen- | te volume named the myrrour of the world or thy- | mage of the same, | [*etc.*]. Leaf 3ᵃ. ◖ Prologue declaryng to whom this book apperteyneth, | [*etc.*]. Leaf 4ᵇ. ◖ Hier begynneth the booke callyd the Myrrour of the | worlde. And treateth first of the power and puyssaunce | of god, Capitulo primo. | [*etc.*]. Leaf 87ᵃ, line 30. ... whiche book I began first to translate the second | day of Ianyuer the yere of our lord, M.CCCC.lxxx. [Leaf 87ᵇ, line 1.] And fynysshyd the viij day of Marche the same yere ; And | the xxi yere of the most Crysten kynge . Kyn | ge Edward the fourthe . Vnder the shadowe of whos noble | proteccion I haue emprysed and fynysshed this sayd lytyl | werke and boke. [*etc.*]   Line 14.   ◖ Caxton me fieri fecit.

Collation.   a–l⁸ ; 88 leaves.   31–2 lines.   No headlines or numbers to pages.

Leaf 1ᵃ–2ᵇ Table, 3ᵃ–4ᵃ Prologue, 4ᵇ–87ᵃ Text, 87ᵃ–87ᵇ Epilogue, 88ᵃ blank, 88ᵇ Caxton's device.   [*B.L.*]   [**1941**¹.]

—— The mirror of the world.
                              fol.   *Lawrence Andrewe.   London* [1527.]

Title.   The myrrour | & dyscrypcyon of the worlde with many meruaylles. | As Gramayre, Rethoryke wyth the arte of memorye, Logyke, Geome- | trye, wyth the standarde of mesure & weyght, & the knowlege how a man | sholde mesure londe, borde, & tymber, & than Arsmetryke wyth the ma- | ner of accoūtes and rekenynges by cyfres, and than Musyke, and Astro- | nomye, with many other profytable and plesant comodytes. | [Woodcut.]   Leaf 92ᵃ *Colophon.*   ◖ Enprynted by me Laurence Andrewe dwel | lynge in fletestrete, at the sygne of the goldē | crosse by flete brydge, | ◖ Cum gratia et priuilegio illustrissimi regis.

Collation.   a–f, +, g–y⁴ ; 92 leaves.   40 lines.   No headlines or numbers to pages.

Leaf 1ᵃ Title, 1ᵇ Woodcut, 2ᵃ Prologue, 2ᵇ Woodcut, 3ᵃ–4ᵃ Table, 4ᵇ blank, 5ᵃ–90ᵇ Text, 91ᵃ Woodcut, 91ᵇ, 92ᵃ Table, 92ᵇ Device. [*B.L.*]   [**1941**².]

VIRGILIUS MARO (PUBLIUS).   The thirteen bukes of Eneados.
                        4to.   [*William Copland.*]   *London*, 1553.

Title [within border].   ✒ THE | . xiii . Bukes of Eneados of | the famose Poete Virgill | Translatet out of Latyne | verses into Scottish me- | tir, bi the Reuerend Fa- | ther in God, May- | ster Gawin Douglas | Bishop of Dunkel & | vnkil to the Erle | of Angus . Euery | buke hauing hys | perticular | Prologe. | ¶ Imprinted at Londō | 1553.

Collation.   [1] A–Z, a–z, aa–bb⁸ ; 385 leaves.   34 lines.   With headlines and numbers to pages.

Leaf 1ᵃ Title, 1ᵇ blank, 2ᵃ–9ᵇ Preface, 10ᵃ–384ᵇ Text, 385 blank. [*B.L.*]   [**1652**.]

VORAGINE (JACOBUS DE). The golden legend.
fol. *Wynkyn de Worde. London,* 1527.

Begins leaf 2ᵃ. ❡ Here foloweth a lytell table contey | nynge the lyues and hystoryes short- | ly taken out of the byble. | [*etc.*]. Leaf 438ᵃ *Colophon.* THus endeth the legende, named in latyn Legēda aurea | that is to saye in englysshe the golden legende. For lyke | as golde passeth all other metalles, so this boke excedeth | all other bokes, wherin ben conteyned all the hygh and | grete feestes of our lorde, the feestes of our blyssed lady, | the lyues, passyons, and myracles of many other sayn- | tes hystoryes and actes, as all alonge here afore is made mencyon, whi | che werke hath ben diligētly amended in diuers places where as grete | nede was. Finysshed the . xxvi . daye of` August, the yere of our lord . M. | CCCCC . xxvii . the . xix . yere of the regne of our souerayne lorde kynge | Henry the eyght. Imprynted at London in Fletestrete at the sygne of | the sonne, by wynkyn de worde.

Collation. A–F⁸, G⁶, a–z, &·, 2, ⁹, aa–yy⁸; 438 leaves. 46 lines. With headlines and numbers to pages.

Leaf 1ᵃ blank, 1ᵇ Woodcut, 2ᵃ–53ᵃ Old Testament histories, 53ᵃ–54ᵇ Table, 55ᵃ–438ᵃ Golden Legend, 438ᵃ Colophon. 438ᵇ W. de Worde's device 12. **[2040.]**

This copy wants leaves 1–3, 7, 8, and the last leaf, and many margins are damaged. It has been made up with manuscript, and copies of Caxton's prologues have been added at the end. *See* " Diary," Apr. 10, 1668.

WEDNESDAY'S FAST.
4to. *Wynkyn de Worde.* [*Westminster,* 1500.]

Title. ❡ Here beginneth a lytel treatyse that she | weth how euery man & woman ought | to faste and absteyne them from flesshe | on yᵉ wednes- day. | [Four woodcuts.] Leaf 4ᵇ, line 5. The whiche he vs graunte, that hanged on yᵉ rode | Cryste that vs bought, with his precyous blode | AMEN | [W. de Worde's device 4.]

Collation. [a⁴]; 4 leaves. 29 lines. No headlines or numbers to pages.

Leaf 1ᵃ Title, 1ᵇ–4ᵇ Text. [*B.L.*] **[1254³.]**

The four woodcuts on the title-page depicting the Infant Christ holding an orb, and three saints, are from the set used in the Sarum Horae, *c.* 1494.

Another edition of this book was printed in 1532, and the two copies known were found in the binding of a book in Merton College, Oxford. One was kept by the college, and the other, presented to Lord Spencer, is now in the Rylands Library, Manchester.

This is the only copy known, and was sold (in the same lot as the unique Foundation of the Chapel of Walsingham) at R. Smith's sale in 1682.

WHITFORD (RICHARD).   The pipe or tun of perfection.
4to.   *Robert Redman.   London*, 1532.

Title.   ℂ Here begynneth the | boke called the Pype, or Tonne, of the | lyfe of perfection.   The reason or cause | wherof dothe playnely appere | in the processe. | [Woodcut.]   Leaf 224^b *Colophon.*   ℂ Imprynted at lon- | don in Fletestrete, by me Robert Red- | man, dwellynge in saynt Dunstones pa- | rysshe, next the churche.   In the yere | of our lorde god a thousande | fyue hondred and . xxxii . | The . xxiii . day of | Marche. | * | ℂ Cum priuilegio | Regali, | [Type ornament].

Collation.   AB⁴, C–V⁸/⁴, X⁸, AA⁴, BB–RR⁸/⁴, ✠² ; 226 leaves.   33–34 lines.   With headlines and numbers to pages.

Leaf 1ᵃ Title, 1ᵇ To the reader, 2ᵃ–3ᵇ Preface, 4ᵃ–224ᵇ Text, 225, 226 Faults escaped.   [*B.L.*]   [**1036²**.]

Copies of this book vary in the last sheet, and some copies (as that in the Huth Library) have Wynkyn de Worde's name in place of Redman's. It is uncertain, therefore, whether it was printed by Redman or De Worde.

Wants all the upper part (text) of Title and leaves 53–56.

WILLIAM OF TYRE.   Belli sacri historia.
fol.   *N. Brylinger and J. Oporinus.   Basle*, 1549.

Title.   BELLI SACRI HI | storia, Libris XXIII comprehen | SA, DE   HIEROSOLYMA,   AC   TERRA   PROMIS | sionis, [*etc.*] . . . GVLIELMO   TYRIO   METROPOLITANO | quondam Archiepiscopo, ac regni eiusdem | Cancellario, autore. | . . . BASILEAE.   Leaf 305ᵇ *Colophon.*   BASILEAE   PER   NICOLAVM   BRYLIN- | GERVM   ET IOANNEM OPORINVM, | Anno salutis humanæ MDXLIX. | Mense Martio.

Collation.   α β⁸ , a–z, A–Z, Aa⁶ Bb⁸ ; 306 leaves.   45 lines.   With headlines and numbers to pages.

Leaf 1ª Title, 1ᵇ Micaelus Toxites ad lectorem, 2ª–7ª Epistola, 7ᵇ–8ª Verses, 8ᵇ blank, 9ª–16ª Index, 16ᵇ blank, 17ª–18ª To the readers, 18ᵇ–305ᵇ Text, 306 blank. [*R.L.*]   [**2270¹.**]

Contains the autograph of " Thomas lorde Wentworth."

WOLSEY (THOMAS).   Gypsuychianae scholae praeceptoribus oratio.
8º. [*Antwerp.*] [1534.]

Leaf 2 begins. ✍ THOMAS | CARDINALIS EBORACEN, &c. | Gypsuychianæ scholæ Præceptoribus | S.D. | [*etc.*].   Ends leaf 4ᵇ. ... uos modo pergite, ac pa- | triam bene merentem honestissi- | mis studiis illustrate.

Collation. A⁴ ; 4 leaves. 28 lines. No headlines or numbers to pages. [*Ital.*]   [**424⁴.**]

This was frequently printed as a single quire to prefix to the Editio of Colet and Rudimenta Grammatices of Lily.   It contains rules and instructions to the masters of the school founded by the Cardinal at Ipswich.

Wants leaf 1.

INDEX OF PRINTERS

(Arranged under Towns)

* The only copy known of book or edition.

I.—ENGLISH AND SCOTTISH PRESSES

(Westminster, London, St. Albans, Edinburgh.)

WESTMINSTER.

PRINTER	DATE	HEADING	PAGE
CAXTON, William	1482	Chronicles	16
	1482	Higden	32
	[1483]	Cessolis	14
	[1484]	Chaucer	15
	1489	Christine de Pisan	15
	[1489]	*Reynard the Fox	54
	[1490]	Vincentius	69
DE WORDE, Wynkyn	[1492]	Chastising of God's Children	15
	[1493]	Treatise of Love	68
	[1495]	Bartholomaeus	5
	1495	*Introductorium Linguae Latinae	34
	1496	Berners	6
	1499	Donatus	20
	[1499]	*Rote or Mirror	55
	[1500]	*Wednesday's Fast	71

(*See* also under LONDON.)

LONDON.

PRINTER	DATE	HEADING	PAGE
ANDREWE, Lawrence	[1527]	Vincentius	70
BANKES, Richard	[?]	*Assize of Bread	1
BERTHELET, Thomas	[?]	Ockham	51
	[1530]	St. Germain	56
	1532	*Elyot	21
	[1532]	Erasmus	22
	1533	St. Germain	57
	1542	Elyot	21
	1543	Henry VIII	29
	1543, etc.	Statutes	59–64
BYDDELL, John	1534	Barnes	4
—— —— *for* William MARSHALL	1534	Of the Old God	51
—— —— ——	1535	*Liturgies.*—Primer	44
—— —— ——	1535	Savonarola	57
CALY, Robert	1555	*Liturgies.*—Breviarium Sarum	42
	1557	Edgeworth	20
CAWOOD, John	1555	Bonner (two works)	11
—— —— *for* J. WALLEY and R. TOTTELL	1557	More	50
—— —— (*see* GRAFTON, Richard)			

PRINTER	DATE	HEADING	PAGE
COPLAND, William	[1548]	Borde	12
	1553	Virgilius	70
	[1555]	Rutter of the Sea	56
	1557	Malory	48
CROWLEY, Robert	1550	Langland	35
DAY, John	[1555]	Bale	4
—— —— and William SERES	[1550]	Hooper	33
DE WORDE, Wynkyn	1502	Le Fevre	36
	1506	Ordinary	52
	[1507]	*Justes of May and June	34
	1509	Fisher	23
	1509	*Liturgies.*—Manuale	48
	1510	Flower of the Commandments	24
	[1510]	*Hawes	28
	1527	Voragine	71
	1530	Bonaventura	11
GRAFTON, Richard	1543	Harding	28
	1548	*Liturgies.*—Prayer	41
	1549	*Liturgies.*—Bk. Common Prayer	39
	1550	*Liturgies.*—Bk. Common Prayer	39
	1550	Halle	27
	1551	*Liturgies.*—Thanksgiving	41
	1552	*Liturgies.*—Order of St. Bart.	40
—— —— and John CAWOOD	1548, etc.	Statutes	64–66
—— —— and E. WHITCHURCH	1539	Bible	6

PRINTER	DATE	HEADING	PAGE
PYNSON, Richard—*contd.*	[1496]	*Skelton	57
	[1496]	*Stanbridge	58
	[1498]	*Donatus	19
	1498	Sulpitius	66
	[1499]	*Informatio Puerorum	33
	1503	*Liturgies.*—Ordinale Sarum	46
	[1505]	Statutes	59
	[1506]	*Bonaventura	10
	1507	Royal Book	55
	[1508]	Carmelianus	14
	1513	Lidgate	37
	1520	*Liturgies.*—Missale	45
	1525	Froissart	25
RASTELL, John	1532	Heywood	31
RASTELL, William	1533	Heywood (two works)	30, 31
	1533	More	50
	1534	Heywood	31
RAYNALD, Thomas, and John HARRYNGTON	1549	Bible	7
REDMAN, Robert	1532	Whitford	72
SERES, William (*see* DAY, John)			
SUTTON, Henry (*see* KINGSTON, John)			
TOTTELL, Richard	1554	Lidgate	37

II.—FOREIGN PRESSES.

(Antwerp, Basle, Caen, Florence, Freiburg, Gouda, Lyons, Milan, Paris, Rome, Strasburg, Valencia, Wittenberg, Zurich.)

ANTWERP.

ANTWERP—*continued.*

PRINTER	DATE	HEADING	PAGE
DE KEYSER, Martin	1535	Dialogues	19
	1535	Lily	38
VAN BERGHEN, Adriaen	1503	Arnold	1

ANTWERP (called Marlborow).

LUFT, Hans	1528	Tindale	67

BASLE.

BRYLINGER, N., and J. OPORINUS	1549	Herold	30
	1549	William of Tyre	72
EPISCOPIUS, Nicolaus	1557	Budé	13
OPORINUS, Joannes	1551	Bible	6

CAEN.

HOSTINGUE, Laurens	1510	Grand Coutumier	17

FLORENCE.

	[1526]	Verini	69
IUNTAE, Philippi, Haeredes	1521	Politi	53

FREIBURG.

FABER, Joannes	1534	Erasmus	22

GOUDA.

LEEU, Gerard	1481	Dialogus	18

LYONS.

PRINTER	DATE	HEADING	PAGE
FRELLON, Jean	1549	Bible	8
ROVILLIUS, Gulielmus	1552	Medina	49
	1557	Cardanus	13
TRECHSEL, M. and G.	1536	Estienne	23
VINCENTII, S., Haeredes	1536	Baif (two works)	3
	1537	Baif	2

MILAN.

DA PONTE, Gotardo	1517	Torniello	68

PARIS.

ASCENSIUS, J. Badius	1508	Geoffrey of Monmouth	26
BONHOMME, Yolande	1532	*Liturgies.*—Primer	43
—— ——	1532	*Liturgies.*—Psalter	47
DE LA BARRE, Nicholas	1498	*Perottus	52
ESTIENNE, Charles	1553	Baif	3
—— Robert	1549	Baif	2
FERREBOUC, Jacques	1521	Cronica	18
LE NOIR, Philippe	[1530]	Le Blazon	9
REGNAULT, Francis	1530	*Liturgies.*—Horae	43
VOSTRE, Simon	[1515]	*Liturgies.*—Horae	41

ROME.

PRINTER	DATE	HEADING	PAGE
BLADUS, Antonius	1525	Fiori	23
FRANCK, Marcel	1523	Eckius	20
GUILLIRETUS, Stephanus	1521	Henry VIII	29

STRASBURG.

SCHOTT, Johan	1548	Krantz	35

VALENCIA.

DIAZ, Francisco	1539	Consulado de Mar	17

WITTENBERG.

LUFT, Hans	1547	Marcort	49

[ZURICH.]

FROSCHOVER, Christopher	[1554]	Turner	68

[Unknown: *France.*]

		Kalendar	35

Lightning Source UK Ltd.
Milton Keynes UK
UKHW010751030620
364295UK00001B/17

9 781108 002042